The Deconstructionists Playbook

AN ANTHOLOGY

Edited by
CRYSTAL CHEATHAM & THERESA TA

Bemba Press
PHILADELPHIA

Bemba Press
An imprint of Our Bible, Inc.
Philadelphia

First edition Published May 2021

Printed in the United States of America

For information about special discounts for bulk purchases, please contact Bemba Press at hi@ourbibleapp.com or visit our website at www.ourbibleapp.com.

ISBN 978-1-7370884-4-8 (Paperback)
ISBN 978-1-7370884-5-5 (Hardcover)

To Anne —
who loved and saw the vision before anyone else.

To Sharon, Keisha, Melvin, & Micky —
for dogged support and cheerleading in the darkest night.

To Nhu & Lan —
for preparing the way behind you with generous freedom to roam.

To Grace, Abby, & Lizzy —
for listening with patient love when it mattered most.

To anyone wishing you had something like this years ago —
We are so glad you've made it here with us now.

To our 1,571 Kickstarter backers —
Together, we've started something bigger than we can ever know.

CONTENTS

PREFACE

Over the last few years, we've been on a journey, figuring out what it means to call oneself a Christian when Christianity itself doesn't want to call you a Christian. Where can you go when the Church and its people stop making space for you? You with your questions that challenge doctrine, your unfamiliar identities, the ways you love and learn from those who do not proclaim Jesus Christ as Lord. *exactly sums it up!*

We wanted to see what could be possible if only folks had the opportunity to explore their questions outside the confines of a churched vacuum. So, we started collecting daily devotionals, scholarly essays, and personal reflections from people asking the same questions: *Where do I go from here? Where do I belong? Can I call myself a Christian anymore? Am I a Christian anymore?*

Then we published them on Our Bible App for the world to see. And we kept going.

Maybe like mad scientists, we didn't know what could come of the steady work; all we knew was that we needed to find out. Eventually, it became apparent that our unprecedented library of devotionals on a phone app was doing some good for an entire community of spiritually unmoored folks. These were — *are* — devotionals no one had ever expected to read on their Bible app. Devotionals meeting people in their doubts, in their church-derived pain, their real anger towards God, or their distress in the absence of a God.

We wanted to create a platform for faith literature that does not shy away from the truths that could make us run far, far away from our churches. Some of our authors hold MDivs and doctorates in the field, and many more do not. But we've established a space where what truly matters—

more than anything else—is that we tell the truth about a personal, lived theology formed from our own experience of the Divine. Because we believe in a God who doesn't require you to base decisions about your spiritual journey on the theologies of some renowned old men.

So, we thought, how can we reach more people who want or need to liberate their spiritual journey? And what if we could create some kind of guide, a playbook of sorts, to help them weave in and out of the treacherous meanderings of faith deconstruction? What if we could compile that very playbook with selections from our library of devotionals?

Wouldn't that be incredibly presumptuous of us to think we could sum it all up for you in these 200 some pages, then just dust off our hands feeling like the work is done? Yes. Incredibly presumptuous. That's why we want you to know that this book is incomplete. It could never truly be finished without more perspectives, more voices, more pages. Hundreds, thousands, millions more.

We do not want you to pick up this book and think, "This is it. This has all the answers I need." Because we *don't* have all the answers—far from it. We don't even have all the questions! This is an incomplete project we hope to never be able to finish, to never run out of contributing voices sharing their perspective of the Divine. So though we don't have all the answers for you, we believe we've compiled—at the very least—a soft place to begin.

This project was born out of love and experience and longing for a God who's just gotta be bigger than the one so many of us have been told exists instead—that God of clichés and platitudes, of checked-off boxes and to-don't lists, of thoughts and prayers with no action. If, after deconstructing your beliefs, you find that your faith in God is strengthened or restored—good for you. And if, after deconstructing your beliefs, you find yourself landing far outside of Christianity—good for you too. So let's begin.

We invite you in,
Crystal Cheatham & Theresa Ta

I · DECONSTRUCTION

Deconstruction is a liberating process of surveying all the elements of one's faith in order to decide which to keep, which to reimagine, and which to completely throw away. As we mature in our faith, we come across parts of Christianity that don't fit with our developing worldview, and this fractures our belief. The deconstruction process requires both courage and community.

This section is here to provide you with a launchpad from which you can start deconstructing toxic theologies that have harmed many and continue to harm more. May your deconstruction, which often feels like an impossible burden, be made lighter by this community of authors who offer their own doubts and reflections on the Bible, God, church, and religion.

We invite you in.

"Theology Ball and Chain"
DAVID HAYWARD

CHAPTER 1
The Paradoxical Necessity of Doubt

Doubt is good.

I view faith and spirituality as a spectrum. The idea that we are all moving back and forth along this shiny golden river, through shallow rocky beds and deeps so far reaching has me smitten with a God who is confident in Their own omnipresence. Just as the Psalmist proclaims in Psalm 139, where can we go that God isn't already there? I really do believe there isn't a single place, not a single situation, where we can't find God — even in our deepest doubts about God Themself.

What if embracing your doubt isn't like relinquishing your faith to the darkness, but rather *letting the light in?* If we see faith as a river we wade into instead of a ladder with a fixed destination, we can better honor each other's processes. There aren't "good Christians" or "bad Christians" anymore. There doesn't even have to be Christians or non-Christians. We can also abolish the tired old "backsliding" narrative and, in its place, choose to honor each person's journey to know God—more ways to identify who/ what/where/ when/how God *is* rather than ways God *isn't.*

The following devotional selections take on doubt in an attempt to arrest its forbiddenness from you. Let your doubt be discernment.

We invite you in.

RECLAIMING THE PURITY OF OUR DOUBT
JESSICA KANTROWITZ

In evangelicalism and other Christian circles, there has been an increasing emphasis over the last century on the importance of believing the "right" doctrine. While this has long been an aspect of Christianity, it has led to our error of defining faith as intellectual belief, rather than trust.

In the United States in particular, as Christianity has become tied to political party lines, more and more things have been added to what you must believe in order to "be a Christian." It is even taught in some churches that true faith will prevent suffering; therefore, if you are suffering in some way, it is because you do not have enough faith.

But true faith is not about signing off on a set of beliefs. Faith is a decision to put your life in God's hands in the same way a small child holds the hand of a trusted adult while crossing the street. Faith is belief that God is with us, somehow, despite pain and suffering, and that none of those things will be left unredeemed.

Faith is believing IN God, not ABOUT God. Faith holds doubt within itself and gives us freedom to hold our own doubts within our faith. We don't have to be afraid that we are sinning by questioning. If truth is truth, it will hold up to our questions. God is not disappointed in us for doubting—God expects our doubt and embraces it, knowing it will ultimately make us stronger.

Do you have doubts or questions that have been making you feel imperfect or impure? What would it look like to accept those questions as part of your faith instead of a challenge to your faith? Can you imagine yourself as a child, slipping your hand into that of God as a trusted parent or friend? Imagine God holding your hand in unconditional love as you ask your questions—not letting go, not getting angry, but listening carefully.

Reclaim the purity of your questions. Reclaim the purity of your struggle to believe and your fear that you don't.

Reclaim the purity of your doubt.

This devotion was adapted from
"Reclaiming Our Purity"
by Jessica Kantrowitz

Unbelief
Erin Green

Thomas, the one called Didymus, one of the Twelve, wasn't with the disciples
when Jesus came. The other disciples told him,
"We've seen the Lord!"
But he replied, "Unless I see the nail marks in his hands,
put my finger in the wounds left by the nails, and put my hand
into his side, I won't believe."
John 20:24-25 (CEB)

Jesus's disciple Thomas is experiencing a tremendous amount of grief, anger, and disbelief John 20. His feelings are reasonable and justified; Jesus was just viciously executed. Thomas's hopes were crushed. Some women reported to have seen the resurrected Jesus; some of the disciples had as well, but Thomas wasn't buying it.

Mother (now Saint) Teresa—an iconic figure of love, sacrifice, and service—also had moments of excruciating disbelief, a complete inability to muster faith. Attempts have been made to hide letters she wrote about her feelings of disbelief because they displayed a raw truth that no person of faith would want to admit to the Church.

Church renderings on the above portion of the Gospel text often dub Thomas's story as the "Doubting Thomas" story. These renderings use the story of Thomas as an example of why we should never be in a state of disbelief when it comes to God. But Thomas's reaction is not an anomaly. Peter denied knowing Jesus three times; Jesus's disciples constantly struggled with having faith; and almost all of the major figures in scripture undergo this kind of spiritual crisis—multiple times. It's normal.

I went through it too. In fact, as someone with a degree in Biblical Studies and as a current MDiv student, I face recurring dilemmas within the text that challenge my presuppositions about God and what I have been taught through immersion and tradition. This is a recurring experience for me. There is nothing wrong with that. Churches and teachers who demonize experiences of doubt and disbelief are demonizing a critical aspect of the human experience. It's unhelpful, and it changes nothing.

Thomas's disbelief was real. And the only thing that could change his mind was to literally touch the wounds Jesus's body That's just what Thomas needed. A few days later, Jesus showed up for Thomas—right in the middle of his crisis of belief—and Thomas was able to touch those wounds.

Doubt and disbelief are integral parts of our transformations as humans. They are the moments we are most fragile, malleable, and aching for truth. We are granted an enormous amount of permission by God to search, doubt, question, and repeat. As a result, I have been able to keep my faith intact. When I have done these things—the doubting, searching, questioning—I've found that not only does God respond, but it's also different each time. And each time, it has been in some exact way that I have needed it to be.

Creator God,
You have fashioned us in love, in tender mercy, in mindfulness, and in compassion.
Help us to never be afraid to doubt or have a crisis of belief.
Use those transformational moments in our lives to show up exactly in
the ways that you know we need.

This devotion was adapted from
"The Most Unconventional Ways of Experiencing God"
by Erin Green

WHAT IF I AM WRONG?

SHANNON CASEY

In Kathryn Schulz's 2011 TED talk "On Being Wrong," she begins with the premise that in general, in an abstract sense, we all understand that we could be wrong. We are even occasionally willing to admit that we have been wrong in the past. After all, everybody makes mistakes, right? We're human. We're fallible.

As her audience agrees to this, she then asks, "What does it feel like to be wrong?" They give her predictable answers: Dreadful. Embarrassing. Thumbs down. That makes sense, we think. Nobody enjoys being wrong.

But then there's a twist! Schulz points out, "You guys are answering the question: 'How does it feel to *realize* you're wrong?' Just being wrong... *feels like being right!*"

Being wrong feels like being right. This conclusion is pretty humbling. If being wrong feels exactly like being right, chances are we're probably all wrong about something we believe right now. Maybe we're even wrong about something we feel certain about.

When we're open to considering that we might be wrong about some of the things we believe, we place ourselves in a position from which we can grow.

People generally resist change in their lives, including change in one's beliefs. But if I still believed in everything exactly the same way I believed it ten years ago, it would be disappointing. I want to learn. I want to grow.

When it comes to theology, no one gets everything right. Therefore, admitting that we might be wrong can be a helpful first step as we enter into conversations about God, the Bible, and the myriad of topics that intersect with our spirituality.

When we are able to come to the table with a posture of humility and curiosity, we can have much more productive and respectful conversations about potentially contentious topics.

This devotion was adapted from
"What If I Am Wrong?"
by Shannon Casey

ACCEPTING THE JOURNEY
CHASE DOST

When I first admitted I wasn't a Christian anymore, I felt guilty.

I was in my final year of seminary on the ordination track, yet my own theology doomed me. For years, I had flirted with the boundaries of orthodoxy, rationalizing my arguably heretical beliefs and defining for myself what it meant to be a Christian. I wanted to make it work—until, one day, I realized I didn't anymore.

I no longer wanted to be a Christian.

This was a problem; everyone was expecting me to graduate, get ordained, and become a pastor. I'd been working toward ordination for the past six years; walking away at that point felt like throwing away my hard-earned degree and running off into the wilderness at the eleventh hour. I had no back-up plan. What was I qualified to do, other than the job to which I'd devoted all those years of training?

For a long time, my response to this fear and uncertainty was denial. I did my best to ignore the insistent intrusion of disbelief, the ever-present voice punctuating my classes and internships with "You don't believe in this. You don't even want to believe in this. Why are you doing this?"

I felt trapped on my path. I was afraid of disappointing those who had affirmed and supported me, afraid of having to figure out a future I thought I'd figured out a long time ago.

Still, there were good moments. There were beautiful, faith-affirming moments of love and hope and grace that reminded me of what had drawn me to pastoral ministry in the first place. I loved God, after all. Even in the midst of my theological woes, that had never changed. It was Jesus and the gospel that gave me pause, not the God of the Hebrew Bible who relentlessly pursued Israel, who overflowed with mercy and compassion, who has redeemed and will redeem. But I was in seminary, heading for Christian ordination. For me, being a Christian meant at least wanting to believe in Christ.

Realizing I no longer wanted to be a Christian was a turning point. Doubt is normal (yes, even for pastors), but this was more than just standard doubting. I felt that there would be no integrity in my ordination, because I believe the Church deserves pastors who *want* the gospel to be true. I knew I had to accept where I was and own up to it, even though it was scary—even though it meant embracing the wilderness.

Faith is a journey. Before any journey can begin, you need to know where you're starting from. Being honest about your doubts, about where you are—and accepting it—is an important first step in any journey of faith or self-understanding.

Sometimes, recognizing where you are can help you see the road map in front of you, final destination included. But sometimes, that self-recognition only shows you the next step, and beyond that—the unknown.

In the Bible, the wilderness is a dangerous place; you don't know what you'll encounter there. But it's also a place of transformation. It is a place where we meet God, a place where we are called into a deeper relationship with both God and each other. Willingly following God out of safety and comfort into the wilderness is a profound act of faith.

God of the wilderness, help us accept where we are on the journey. Embolden us to put our trust in you, to follow even when we cannot yet see what comes next.

This devotion was adapted from
"Embracing the Journey"
by Chase Dost

THE POWER OF DOUBT

AMANDA GAYLE REED

> *Thomas, the one called Didymus, one of the Twelve, wasn't with*
> *the disciples when Jesus came. The other disciples told him,*
> *"We've seen the Lord!"*
> *But he replied, "Unless I see the nail marks in his hands,*
> *put my finger in the wounds left by the nails, and put my hand*
> *into his side, I won't believe."*

John 20:24-25 (CEB)

Doubting Thomas doesn't really get the attention he deserves in our churches. The story of Thomas is often reserved for the Sunday after Easter, a day we preachers associate with low attendance and falls victim to the post-Holy Week exhaustion of those called to proclaim the Word. But Thomas's story is important—too important to shrug off as a Resurrection story afterthought.

Thomas wasn't with his friends that particular day. They were still in hiding during the aftermath of the Crucifixion. Mary Magdalene had encountered the Risen Christ at the tomb and, at his request, had gone and told the disciples. Exactly what they thought of her response, we don't know—not from the recording in the Gospel of John, anyhow. But it seems as if they didn't believe her, because the next thing we hear is that they are hiding in a locked room, in fear of the authorities, when Jesus suddenly appears to them.

Thomas isn't there. He doesn't see the miracle. He isn't a part of the holy moment, though his friends try to persuade him that it had really happened. Finally, Thomas gushes forth with a skepticism and doubt to which I've always related: "Unless I see the nail marks in his hands, put my finger in the wounds... I won't believe." (v. 25).

Growing up with my science teacher father, I learned pretty early to meet unlikely stories with a bit of skepticism. I was taught and encouraged to ask questions from an early age. We often debated philosophical, theological, and political issues at the dinner table. We wondered, observed, and—like any scientist—we searched for the objective proof.

That Thomas needed to see and experience this miracle for himself doesn't strike me as evidence of a weak faith. On the contrary, he strikes me as one with a *tremendous* faith.

He had faith in a God who promised to be present, a God who said, "ask and you shall receive." Thomas had faith in a God who would hear the question and would answer. This is not an easy thing to do in our world.

I, too, am someone who needs to see and experience the Divine. I've spent my life seeking answers to questions. Usually, those answers just lead me to deeper questions. On more than one occasion, when I've asked what seemed to be obvious questions, I was called a "Doubting Thomas." But it is that doubt which has encouraged me to wrestle with faith so that my spirit grows stronger and stronger. Doubt draws us out of the realm of blindly believing and into an experiential faith in which we encounter, in our lives, the Risen Christ.

Doubt is not a weakness. Doubt is a tool.

This devotion was adapted from
"The Power of Doubt"
by Amanda Gayle Reed

MEETING CHRIST
IN AGNOSTIC DOUBT
REV. DREW TUCKER

There's a bogus narrative, promoted by the "God's Not Dead" version of Christianity, that colleges and universities are places where faith isn't safe because some militant Atheists and Agnostics are out to wreck the precious faith of fragile young adults.

I don't say it's bogus because there aren't Atheists or Agnostics on college campuses; in fact, I'm very well acquainted with a number of them on the campus where I work. They're my colleagues. They're my friends. It's a bogus narrative because, at the seven colleges I've been a part of since 2005, precious few of the Atheists or Agnostics I encountered were out to destroy other peoples' faith.

The people most commonly challenging faith assumptions in the classroom were theologians, pastors, and professors of religion—not seeking to eradicate faith, but to deepen engagement by challenging assumptions. The people most militant about their faith, the most confrontational, were fundamentalists and other conservative evangelicals.

And though they're often lumped together, there's a significant difference between Atheism and Agnosticism. Atheists believe that there is no God or gods. Agnostics say there isn't enough evidence to prove or disprove spiritual beings, a divine realm, or the existence of G/god(s). In short, Agnostics lean into skepticism while taking seriously the limitations of human knowledge, including their *own* knowledge.

For a long time, my faith practice was entirely a mental enterprise. As a philosophy major and summa cum laude graduate of Ashland University, I entered seminary as an overconfident twenty-something.

Then, I took my first Old Testament exam, which I summarily failed. This launched me into a faith crisis, which became the first sign of my own deconstruction. If I couldn't mentally grasp the logic of this faith, the reasonability of God's existence, and Christianity's truth—then either I was a failure, or my faith was false. So the logic went in my head, at least.

Too many Christians have been told that doubt or disbelief are sins or, at the very least, evidence of unfaithfulness. This is both contrary to the Bible and ignores the simple meaning of words. After all, faith is a kind of commitment beyond the hard evidence. This means that there's always room for doubt in faith.

That's what I've learned from the Agnostics in my life. In their unwillingness to stake a claim based on insufficient evidence, these friends, colleagues, and peers have revealed to me that faith is, at some level, unreasonable. There are gaps where facts don't hold, and only trust can bridge the ravines. They also helped me see that my struggles to believe don't make me a failure—they make me human, and that doubt is a shared human experience.

Doubt isn't a lack of faith. Indeed, just as the parent who wanted their child healed but couldn't believe it was possible, we cry out, "I have faith; help my lack of faith!" (Mark 9:24, CEB) There is holy space for doubt, and I've learned from my Agnostic friends and colleagues on campus that living in the doubt doesn't mean I've abandoned my faith. It means that, in some areas, I need to lean into trusting rather than rationalizing. And in other areas, where I was so unreasonably certain, it's entirely appropriate to reserve judgment.

Rachel Held Evans once said that she enjoyed saying the Apostles' Creed together in church because, where she struggled to believe some things, other peoples' trust supported her; and in areas where she had confidence, that strength supported others in their doubt. When we share our faith—in doubts and in clarity—we share an honest expression of who we are as people seeking to trust something, someone, beyond the facts and yet at the very core of our beings.

This devotion was adapted from
"Meeting Jesus in Interfaith Relationships"
by Drew Tucker

CHAPTER 2
The Bible

I was raised to believe that the Bible is a historical document. But besides the occasional historical narrative, the Bible is filled with cultural myths, legends, prophecies, and allegories told with much poetic license.

Who among us has never learned something worthwhile from a fictitious tale, felt the pangs of love and heartache in poetic verse, or become more brave—more yourself—after reading the details of a hero's journey?

Still, there was a time I believed that the Bible was more useful as a self-help book, never mind the fairy-tale stories. The Bible was a book of rules I thought I was using to sculpt moralistic views and ethical policies, never mind its many contradictions regarding the correct actions of humanity.

As we deconstruct our faith, how do we grapple with what has been done in the name of the Bible? Slavery, white supremacy, harmful patriarchal systems—all reinforced at the behest of this treasured library of ancient literary works.

If you, like me, are looking for ways to reconcile the things you love about the holy book with your concerns—then hopefully these next devotions will provide useful insight on how they were able to sift through to the truths that this timeless collection of books provides.

We invite you in.

Imagination & the Bible
Laura Jean Truman

Then Moses stretched out his hand over the sea. The Lord pushed the sea back by a strong east wind all night, turning the sea into dry land. The waters were split into two. The Israelites walked into the sea on dry ground. The waters formed a wall for them on their right hand and on their left.
Exodus 14:21-22 (CEB)

Stories lend us fire when we are out of our own. They show us how our story—the sometimes too-small feeling story—fits into a bigger story. When we're tired, stories that speak to our imagination can wake us up, give us courage, give us empathy.

On the day of Donald Trump's inauguration, I curled up in my PJ's, turned off my computer, and had a *Lord of the Rings* marathon. But what does the Bible, a book of rules and religiosity, have to do with imagination? What does a book of facts and numbers and hymns have to do with *Lord of the Rings*?

Well, the Bible is a lot more like *Lord of the Rings* than some may think; just as LOTR helps us enter into sacred time for courage and bravery, the Bible ushers us into sacred time with stories to make us brave.

The first time I seriously considered a non-literal Bible, it was pretty traumatic. I was in graduate school, and we learned that the parting of the Red Sea didn't happen. It felt like I didn't just lose my Bible; I was losing my whole religion.

The Red Sea wasn't parted. There wasn't a tremendous flood. Donkeys didn't talk. My worldview tumbled down and broke like the walls of Jericho didn't. If it isn't true, *what's even the point?*

If it's just a story, the implication is that it's not as valuable. But on inauguration day in 2017, I chose a story. Not as a second choice, but as a first choice. I needed courage to resist fascism, and so I turned to a wizard… sitting with a Hobbit (?) in a dwarf mine (?) while they tried to throw a magical Ring of Power (?!) into the heart of a volcano where the Dark Lord (??) lived with his Big Eye (???). And it was exactly what I needed.

Stories matter. Stories are salvific.

"We meet God in narrative," Rachel Held Evans told us in her fabulous book *Inspired*. God knows that we're a story people. The Bible is a book of stories, not because it is less than a literal book, but because it is *more* than a literal book.

This doesn't mean that everything in scripture is fictional. *Inspired* and Peter Enns's book, *The Bible Tells Me So,* are great introductions to a framework of biblical interpretation that holds space for genre and context, for a book full of stories and also history, a book of letters and also songs.

But our God knows us so well, and God knows that there are things we learn from stories that we can't learn anywhere else. If we start from the premise that we need our imaginations to be awakened, and that willpower isn't enough to keep us going—wouldn't it make sense that God would give us a book of stories for when we get weary?

What kind of a God would give us a book of rules when it's not *rules* that make us braver, kinder, stronger—but *stories*.

God, help us trust that You are good and that you love us.
Help us trust that that means the Bible wasn't written to subdue us,
but to wake us up, give us hope, and give us courage.
Give us eyes to see courage in scripture today.
Amen.

This devotion was adapted from
"Imagination: The Most Underrated Spiritual Discipline"
by Laura Jean Truman

MESSY, SCARY, CONFUSING
VINCE BRUNO

I was brought to the Christian faith by a very loving and very fundamentalist family who taught me that the Bible is the perfect, uncontradictable word of God. The Bible depicts God as the loving and gracious God who is worthy of worship. The Bible is accurate and contains no fallacies. Any problem I may face in life has a solution in the Bible. The Bible is a simple to follow and easy to understand book.

Now, here's the thing: I pride myself on being an open-minded and considerate person. I also admire this family for all they've done for me. So I don't do so lightly when I say that this well-meaning family was absolutely and unequivocally incorrect.

The Bible is *full* of contradictions. There are horrific depictions of God. There are questionable ethics and inaccurate portrayals of science. The Bible is missing a lot of extremely important topics and instead includes a lot of irrelevant ones.

The Bible is a complicated mess that is excruciatingly confusing and difficult to read.

And yet, here we are, still using the book nearly 2,000 years after its most recent texts were written and more than 1,600 years after it was compiled. There has got to be something within its pages, among those atrocious and problematic verses, that makes it worth reading. Somehow, it still points us to a God worthy of worship.

The Bible is a messy, scary, and confusing book. It's been used to justify horrible atrocities in the past and continues to be used in such ways by many people today. So how can we trust it?

I think a starting point is to acknowledge that the Bible is an extremely diverse book. It is a book that has hundreds of writers, written over the course of thousands of years for millions of different readers. And the Bible is incredibly aware of that. The Bible doesn't hide it. The Bible embraces its diversity.

The Bible allows its writers to grow and mature in their faith and doesn't shame them for changing their minds on difficult topics. It presents ancient and creative ideas for how the earth was perceived, not to tell us history, but to fascinatingly express God's loving relationship with Creation.

My old college professor has a great way of looking at the Bible; just as we say that Jesus was fully God and fully human, we can also say that the Bible is fully divine and fully human.

The Bible is messy, just like us. The Bible evolves, just like us. The Bible is atrocious, just like we can be.

It was divinely inspired and was written by humans. It has all the properties of human nature; yet it still points us to a loving God worthy of worship.

This devotion was adapted from
"Problematic Biblical Verses and What to Do with Them"
by Vince Bruno

CHAPTER 3
Church, Religion, & Belief Systems

What now can we say about the Church? That word in itself can be a hydra. When named, it can be an individual church—as in your home church; it can mean something a bit bigger—as in your denomination; or even something larger, an institution—as in The Christian Church; still also, it can mean the community of people who make up any level of these meanings for church.

It is scary to think of how the Church has responded to being challenged or confronted. On one hand, the Church has condoned and continues to condone many of history's greatest atrocities. On the other hand, the Church has offered aid and a home to many without.

Friend or foe, speaking up and challenging the Church can quickly turn into a nightmare, even if it's just quietly to yourself. How do we wrap our minds around the untouchable beast that is The Church?

In the Harry Potter world, there is a magical beast (called a Boggart) that takes on the physical manifestation of its challenger's greatest fear. To banish it (and forgive the nerdiness here), one must instead imagine the Boggart as something amusing, then cast the spell: *Riddikulus*. Only after the fear is replaced with amusement—after the spellcaster realizes the beast has no true control over them—can the Boggart be defeated. Sometimes, in order to snap out of the terror trance we are in, we must make ridiculous the thing we fear the most. We must realize that the beast does not truly have control over us.

The following authors do us the service of dismantling some of the more intimidating parts of church life. Let's allow ourselves to see through the fear—that false control—and discover the ridiculous.

We invite you in.

DEATH OF AN OLD
BELIEF SYSTEM
MEL GARMAN

"Death is a part of life. My prayer for you this season is that you make
time to celebrate that reality, and to grieve that reality,
and that you will know you are not alone."
Rachel Held Evans

Some would say that death is not just physical. It can occur in a multitude of ways: social, emotional, mental, financial, spiritual. For those of us who have left various conservative belief systems behind in pursuit of something more life-giving, we may have experienced a form of death ourselves.

Like Jesus, we may have endured the sting of betrayal from Judas in our own lives—dear former friends who suddenly turned on us. And those dear friends may have turned on us for any number of reasons. Maybe the wrong people found out our sexual orientation. Maybe it started with a simple disagreement with a church leader. It could've begun with a single political article shared on social media that relayed a message similar to Jesus's words to the religious leaders in Mark 7: "You ignore God's commandment while holding on to rules created by humans and handed down to you." (v. 8, CEB). Whatever it was—as with Jesus—the second we didn't toe the party line, it might have led us to becoming disposable pawns in the eyes of certain religious and political institutions.

Many of us who leave belief systems like conservative evangelical Christianity may have paid a price for not conceding to their exclusionary standards. Our backs may have been whipped with the pain of communal loss, our heads adorned with a prickly crown of isolation, our sides stricken with the grief of deconstruction and disillusionment. As with the women who were present for Jesus's crucifixion, the people sitting at our proverbial cross may have been the most unexpected. But in one way or another, we had no choice but to give our former belief system—or parts of it—a final, dying breath in which we uttered, "It is finished."

And with those words, the curtain of our faith-temple was torn from top to bottom. The earth of our worldview shook; the rocks of our certainty split; and the tomb of our personal thoughts released into the public eye.

Lord, help us to realize that peacemaking requires division. That liberation requires disunity. Help us to understand that we can't free the captives without pissing off captors. We can't loosen the chains of injustice without rebelling against jailors. We can't untie the yoke of oppression without disobeying masters. We can't love our neighbors without working to free them from the oppressive chokehold of their enemies, and we can't love our enemies unless we make some first.

This devotion was adapted from
"Reconstruction as Resurrection"
by Mel Garman

IT'S NOT THEIRS TO TAKE
HOPE ZANE

Before I created you in the womb I knew you;
before you were born I set you apart;
I made you a prophet to the nations.
Jeremiah 1:5 (CEB)

At its best, the Church can be a wonderful source of community and support. Unfortunately, the Church isn't always a safe place for everyone. At times, the very human, frail, and fallible people who make up the Church can cause deep wounds that linger for a lifetime, intentional or not. So what do you do when your oppression comes from the Church?

This message is for everyone, but if you've ever been hurt by the Church or by another Christian, it is especially for you: *No one can bar you from the love of God.* You are not too gay for the Church. You are not too queer. You are not too trans. You are not too poor. You are not too brown. You are not too liberal, too conservative, too young or old. You are perfect and beloved.

No matter who you are, who you love, what you have or haven't done, God loves you. Not in spite of who you are, but *because* of who you are. Your Creator shaped and molded every facet of you, down to the most intricate detail. There is nothing about you God does not know. There is nothing God doesn't call beloved, perfect, and holy.

No matter what anyone has ever told you, at any point in your life, they can't take God from you. They can't even take Christianity. It's not theirs to take. Christ's grace and mercy is offered to all, free and clear—no strings attached. Your hurt is real. Your anger is justified. But God loves you, and in God's eyes, you are beloved.

This devotion was adapted from
"In His Name All Oppression Shall Cease"
by Hope Zane

LEAVING TOXIC RELIGION

Chrissy Stroop

Here's a little secret about the relationship between deconstruction and reconstruction: there's no sharp line between the two.

Both are necessary components of healthy, morally autonomous self-cultivation for those whose prior self-formation was inextricably intertwined with toxic religion.

Unpacking that experience, which will always be part of you, takes hard work. It's often painful. But in working toward healing, and in repurposing your evangelical or other toxic religious background to better ends that you choose for yourself, you can find a kind of "redemption" (if that's a metaphor that works for you).

The critical capacities you've cultivated in making your brave move away from toxic religion will continue to serve you well as you look for new sources of meaning and purpose—whether you do so in the context of a progressive faith tradition and healthy religious community or in the context of giving up religion altogether (like I've done). Both paths out of toxic religion are valid; in the exvangelical community, we try to build bridges between people in those two broad groups because all of us who have left toxic religion behind have a lot in common.

Unaddressed trauma can leave us in a similar place of perpetual immaturity. And fundamentalist religion functions systematically to keep us in that state: immature and controllable, with our humanity forced into rigid conformity with a stifling set of beliefs and rules.

Fundamentalism is a misdirected response to trauma, perpetuated communally and generationally. By design, fundamentalism—with its communal and internalized disciplinary mechanisms—becomes intertwined with our egos and identities, making it very difficult to break away. When we do, we're often left feeling adrift. How do we learn who we are and what to want, apart from all of that?

Consider this: In order for you to break away from something as powerful as toxic religion at all, something in you—some inner strength, some part that could not be contained—had to be strong enough to get you to listen to, and then act on, your doubts. This move, which starts you on your way to authentic self-realization, is not the move of a weak person.

This devotion was adapted from
"Redeeming Our Evangelical Upbringings"
by Chrissy Stroop

A SPIRITUAL BURIAL
MEL GARMAN

You yourself have kept track of my misery.
Put my tears into your bottle—
aren't they on your scroll already?
Psalm 56:8 (CEB)

When I was deconstructing my former faith framework, it felt like a part of me died. Unearthing the complex string of lies I was fed about the universe was jarring. As I buried my former faith and laid it to rest, I experienced immense grief. How could I not? Even as someone who still identifies with Christianity, it felt akin to an actual spiritual death.

Leaving a former belief system behind is painful no matter what direction one moves on toward. For many of us, our once unwavering fundamentalist sense of certainty, like a corpse, immediately begins to rot and wither away. Our lifelong devotion to a belief system might start to feel like a fruitless house of cards built on sand. Ideas that were once unquestionably deemed universal truth are now wrought with unknown mysteries, blatant untruths, and rampant oppression.

And oh, how hurtful it is to come to grips with this. Unraveling this web of confusion might have caused us to endure a period of quiet despair, of silent heartache, of profound hopelessness. In fact, we may still be existing in that strange tension between Friday and Sunday—unsure if there was a light at the end of the tunnel after all of this. Uncertain if there is a way to pick up the pieces and recreate them into something new, something healthier, something more beautiful.

During this spiritual burial, people we deeply love may have been mourning outside our proverbial tomb, as well. They may have been grieving in their own way—wondering why we can't just be exactly who they want us to be, why we can't believe the exact concepts they profess. At some point, we may find ourselves on the other side of that tension: Why can't they see there's more to their faith than what they've been told? That there are better, alternative views? Why can't they also see there is no freedom in their belief system? Heartbreak abounds.

Know today that God is near to the broken-hearted and reflect on this phrase:
"The story does not end here."

This devotion was adapted from
"Reconstruction as Resurrection"
by Mel Garman

NOT A RESTRICTION
TYLER MARTIN

Cleaning out my bedroom has always been therapeutic—throwing out what I don't need and, more importantly, what I don't want. As a teenager, without fail, my first roadblock was always when my parents saw what I wanted to throw out: "But you loved that!" "That still fits you!" "Hold on, that's new—you only got that four years ago!"

I've found that deconstruction is no different. It's a long journey of cleaning out what we don't need and want. After we've asked the hard questions, after we've educated ourselves and had the uncomfortable conversations, we're left with a hefty "donation" pile.

Although I thought of it as a roadblock, I must annoyingly admit I now appreciate my parents always stopping me, making me double-check what I wanted to throw out. Without a doubt, I would always find a handful of items I regretted putting in the trash.

Isn't this often true of deconstruction? As angry as I get at the Christian faith, there are still things I absolutely adore about it. And maybe, just maybe, I don't have to completely cast it entirely out of my life.

I am really into tarot cards. Funny enough, I think one reason I'm connected to them is actually because they remind me of Christianity. Almost as if they act as a daily devotional. The packaging looks a little different, but the intentions feel the same—they do for me, anyway. I also have begun using spell, or intention, candles. (The evangelical child inside me still shudders a bit when I admit it. But in reality, it's not all that spooky!)

After I light the candle and say my intention aloud, I sit and meditate on it. Accompanying ceremonial candles with prayer is super common in most religions, including Christianity. It's something that I still love from my Christian faith.

(Imagine me saying this as a parent) *You don't have to throw away everything!*

If you like the format of a Christian prayer, keep it! If you like bread and grape juice (as shocking as that might be), go out and get some from the store! No matter if I use tarot, spell candles, or join some obnoxiously energetic cycling class—for me, Jesus will always be important, and that's just a fact.

Deconstruction isn't a restriction; it's a liberation.

What are the things you love about your religion? Are there ways to keep those things while affirming your full, authentic self? Are there rituals and traditions from other religions or practices that speak to you? Learn about them. Respectfully explore! You don't have to restrict yourself to the religious practices of one tradition. There are plenty of ways to connect to spirit—like being in nature, journaling, listening to music, reading, cooking, having wild sex.

Your options are endless.

This devotion was adapted from
"It's a Choice, It's a Lifestyle"
by Tyler Martin

DECONSTRUCTING HEAVEN

JASON KOON

I heard a loud voice from the throne say, "Look! God's dwelling is here with human-kind. He will dwell with them, and they will be his peoples. God himself will be with them as their God. He will wipe away every tear from their eyes. Death will be no more. There will be no mourning, crying, or pain anymore, for the former things have passed away." Then the one seated on the throne said, "Look! I'm making all things new." He also said, "Write this down, for these words are trustworthy and true." Then he said to me, "All is done. I am the Alpha and the Omega, the beginning and the end. To the thirsty I will freely give water from the life-giving spring. Those who emerge victorious will inherit these things. I will be their God, and they will be my sons and daughters.

Revelation 21:3-7 (CEB)

One night, after picking up my daughter from her new youth group, she told me her youth pastor said that "Jesus was going to come back and burn the whole world up and turn it into hell."

So, we had some work to do.

We read three chapters from the book of Revelation together. Revelation 19-21, straight through—no pauses, no skipping verses. We read about the New Jerusalem coming down out of the clouds, descending to the Earth. We read about the old order of things passing away and a fresh infusion of newness into creation. We read that the dwelling place of God is now with humanity, not the other way around.

And at the end of it all, she said, "So you mean, I'm standing in future heaven right now?"

I nodded.

"I'm not quite sure, but I think that's what it might be saying." Imagine the implications of this kind of paradigm shift. If my ultimate hope is evacuation—soul ripped from body, carried off to a far-away ethereal paradise—then what is the point of anything I do in this life?

Why care for a creation that is destined to burn? Why alleviate suffering among people whose eternal destiny is to become fuel for the fires of a terrifying hellscape?

But if I'm standing in "future heaven," everything that happens here and now is significant. My concern for creation and the work I do to alleviate suffering, poverty, and loneliness has eternal significance. If my final state is both physical as well as spiritual, my emotions, desires, and passions are immediately infused with fresh eternal significance.

Our popular conceptions of heaven as a purely spiritual and distant realm are based more on the ancient Greek philosopher Plato and the fifth-century theologian Augustine than anything else. And while many people still view this imagery as the only legitimate depiction of heaven, a closer look at scripture and tradition tells a different story—or (to be more precise) they allude to several different stories.

An honest look into what might lie beyond the unthinkable reveals varying and nuanced metaphors—seemingly contradictory imagery that is both beautiful and confusing. It will challenge us to rethink metaphors we used to understand as propositional, as well as propositions we once viewed as metaphors. We'll end up slipping out of our former rock-solid certainty and then snicker at the narrowly defined categories with which we used to see the afterlife. In short, it will probably leave us with more questions than answers.

But that's the beauty of deconstruction. We get to ask the questions. We are free to explore the options and then sit in the uncertainty of it all, considering its implications, rather than smothering it under the weight of pat Sunday School answers.

And God might meet us in the uncertainty with a vague hope that goodness and mercy probably await us beyond the unthinkable. This vague hope, which has the power to infuse our here-and-now existence with a fresh jolt of cosmic purpose and eternal significance.

Think about your own ideas of the afterlife. As best as you know, where did they originate from? What about your understanding of eternity have you been uncomfortable with in the past? Are there elements of it that don't make sense?

This devotion was adapted from
"Deconstructing Heaven"
by Jason Koon

DECONSTRUCTING JUDGMENT
JASON KOON

All of you who revere the Lord—praise him!

All of you who are Jacob's descendants—honor him!

All of you who are all Israel's offspring—

stand in awe of him!

Because he didn't despise or detest

the suffering of the one who suffered—

he didn't hide his face from me.

No, he listened when I cried out to him for help.

I offer praise in the great congregation

because of you;

I will fulfill my promises

in the presence of those who honor God.

Let all those who are suffering eat and be full!

Let all who seek the Lord praise him!

I pray your hearts live forever!

Every part of the earth

will remember and come back to the Lord;

every family among all the nations will worship you.

Because the right to rule belongs to the Lord,

he rules all nations.

Psalm 22:23-28 (CEB)

Back when I was a pastor, I used to avoid preaching on heaven, hell, or the book of Revelation like it was the... uhh... plague. It wasn't just the violent judgment imagery and the twisted fascination some Christians seem to approach it with. It wasn't just the endless speculation and interpretive gymnastics of the run-for-the-hills-the-rapture-is-coming crowd. These things were definitely part of the reason, but there was more. "I just don't understand it," I would have said, "I don't know enough to teach this stuff."

As I continue to grow and learn, I am beginning to realize that all theology, to some extent, is autobiographical. In other words, my beliefs don't form in a vacuum, but against a cultural backdrop. Our worldviews are formed in response to real-world questions and curiosities, and the violent imagery of Revelation was no different.

The Book of Revelation was written during a time of intense localized persecution at the hands of what the early Christians saw as an unholy Roman Empire. As a result, their hope for ultimate liberation became intertwined with a vision of God's judgment against their oppressors.

Now, this doesn't mean we can get around the idea of judgment entirely. The judgment motif is sprinkled throughout both scripture and tradition to the point that it's difficult to even read through a single book of the Bible without bumping into it. We can't ignore judgment altogether, but we can recognize that it's not born in violent bloodlust, but out of an intense longing for ultimate liberation.

Almost every vision of the afterlife has, at its core, a longing for and promise of ultimate liberation from sin, pain, and injustice. What does that mean for those who perpetrate these things here and now? I'm not entirely sure, but it doesn't seem promising.

I don't know how we get from the world as it currently is to the world that should be without bumping into judgment along the way. I do know, however, that a God who pours out eternal retribution on anyone who dares to challenge him is not the centerpiece of our hope. Instead, the centerpiece of our eternal hope is the desire for liberation and a hunger for redemption and justice. These things are at the center of God's ultimate plan for humanity, and, more than likely, what awaits us beyond the unthinkable.

This devotion was adapted from
"Deconstructing Heaven"
by Jason Koon

CHAPTER 4
God

If the Almighty wore a name tag, I imagine it might read something like:

GOD (AKA) I AM

they/she/he

At least I would like to believe so. The truth is, I can talk about my perception of God's pronouns, gender, or race all I want, but that doesn't necessarily make it "true." For all of the thousands of years humans have been worshiping a God or gods on this earth, we haven't actually accumulated much factual knowledge about who God is at all. Stranger still, we haven't cracked the code for making God grant every miracle, bestow blessings, save us all from cancer, or interact with us on command.

What I do know is that I have believed for too long in a kind of God that was imagined by older, whiter men than me. And their version of God has repeatedly fallen short of human decency. But the God I meet when I commune with my mother over the phone, when we bow our heads and feel that holy energy coursing through our prayers for family, for safety, and good health? That God makes sense. So which one is it?

Who is this grand, elusive Being who can hold me close through the arms of a loving community one minute, but look away when a pregnant teenager is kicked out of her home and church in the next?

Like Moses, these next authors have dared to stare into the swirling wind and fire, hoping to see a face that belongs to that clear voice of the Divine. Like Thomas and like the Marys, they've clutched at something precious, brought it to the cross, and pleaded, "Father, is this you?"

We invite you in.

How Long, O Lord?

EMILY JOY ALLISON

How long, God, will foes insult you?
Are enemies going to abuse your name forever?
Why do you pull your hand back?
Why do you hold your strong hand close to your chest?
Yet God has been my king from ancient days—
God, who makes salvation happen in the heart of the earth!

Psalm 74:10-12 (CEB)

There's a lot of "How long, O God" statements in the Psalms. This is just one of them. I remember reading a book years ago by that title (*How Long, O Lord* by D. A. Carson) during my time at Moody Bible Institute, which purported to answer the question of theodicy—the question of human suffering: *How can God exist and be both all-powerful and good?*

Sadly, the book is limited by its own worldview, as it cannot conceive of a God that has any space for change of its own or for free will of human beings. The answer that the book, as well as many other books and pastors, comes to is some variation of "IDK how. It just makes sense, so stop asking questions or you're a heretic."

To my way of thinking, belief in a God that truly pulls every puppet string requires relinquishing the belief that humans have any true purpose, meaning, or agency on this earth. It's a tough pill to swallow for some, but I would rather not understand the relationship between my will and the divine fabric of the universe than believe that I have no will or purpose at all beyond mere existence as a cog in the machine of a destiny I cannot change. The truly radical answer to the question "How long, O Lord?" is: *I do not know.*

But I know that God is not the cause of my suffering. I know that God is on the side of the oppressed. I know that God is for human flourishing. I know that God does not inflict suffering on me to teach me a lesson. I know that God is not vindictive. I know that God does not will death or illness or pain or heartbreak or oppression on God's people.

I know that God is working salvation in the earth.

This devotion was adapted from
"Divine Space for Divine Emotions"
by Emily Joy Allison

CHRIST & THE CHURCH

CINDY WANG BRANDT

There is a lot of disillusionment with the Church. People (which the Church consists of) disappoint, and we figure out ways to salvage God's reputation by distancing Godself from the actions of mere mortals.

The dichotomy which arises from the notion that we can experience God outside of our relationship with others in community is a product of Western individualism entrenched in the Protestant salvation narrative. Our entitlement to a personal relationship with God impresses us with a false confidence. We believe we can experience God apart from the works of flawed human beings.

Although there is evidence in scripture of individuals interacting with God directly, the Bible is far more insistent on the way God uses imperfect people to reach others—from the disbelieving Abraham to selfish Kings, to dim-witted disciples, to a violent Paul.

We do not have faith in a vacuum; our faith is always in the context of community. This is why we can't easily separate God from people's ideas about God. When hurt and abuse and disappointment occur within the Church, we can't easily apologize for God, because God has always been about using pathetic people to bring about redemption.

There have always been people kept out of Church by self-righteous gate-keepers (the worst representations of the inclusive Christ). So I get wanting to keep Christ untainted from Christian culture. The Church can be so ugly and devoid of grace. It's just that God has always been a God who taints Himself with the messiness of humanity.

Here's the thing: the Church is made up of a body of broken people. You can be hurt by one part of the body—and I don't want to minimize that hurt—but the hope is that there are other parts of the body who are hurting with you, walking with you through the pain and ready to carry you on their backs whenever you've given up the last bit of energy to keep going.

People are capable of inflicting terrible pain, but they are also vessels for the greatest love. I have never experienced the love of God more than through some ridiculous people who are overly kind or far too generous, with the most tender sensitivity. They insist on believing when all evidence points otherwise and pursue dignity and respect for others at the cost of their own. Some of them identify as Christians, and some don't.

But the God who is Love uses a medley of corresponding voices to whisper the message of hope. Hear the music, from the symphony of community, historical and present.

God sings through God's people.

This devotion was adapted from
"Can We Take Christ Out of the Church?"
by Cindy Wang Brandt

GOD HAS NEVER BEEN A CHRISTIAN

DANNY PRADA

God is Mystery.

The moment we speak a word about God, we are already reducing God to our level of understanding. For this reason, it's always been common for Christians to speak of God as the ineffable one. Augustine once said that "God transcends even the mind." Aquinas made a similar claim when he said that "by its immensity, the divine substance surpasses every form that our intellect reaches." Only those who have been humbled by this transcendent Mystery can truly begin to see the Divine in the lives of those who do not share the same faith they do.

If God cannot be captured by words, then all religious language is necessarily symbolic and limited in its scope. Knowing the inherent limitation of language allows us to expand our notion of truth and who we believe is in possession of it. If God is Ultimate Truth, then Ultimate Truth is beyond anyone's ability to fully capture and box-in.

That is not to say that there is no Absolute Truth, but that no one can ever possess this truth absolutely. All of us are just hinting at that which is far beyond our ability to fully comprehend. A God we can understand is just an idol we've created in our image. A God who is comprehensible is no God at all.

So, if our own particular language about God is limited, would it not be fair to say that the religious language of others can possibly complement and even enhance our own?

If this is true, it makes much more sense for us to hold our beliefs with an open hand instead of a closed fist. The former way enables dialogue; the latter shuts it down. It should be obvious at this point that no one religion can ever claim to dominate the plan of God for the world, including our own.

God has never been a Christian, and though we love our tradition, we must never confine God to it.

This devotion was adapted from
"Above Every Name"
by Danny Prada

GOD CAN TAKE IT
JONAH VENEGAS

Throw all your anxiety onto him, because he cares about you.
1 Peter 5:7 (CEB)

How's your walk with the Lord?

I hate that question. Luckily, no one asks me anymore, but the kind of people who might ask wouldn't like my answer anyway. Maybe I was swearing up and down at God last night. Maybe my journal was filled with expletives and accusations against the Divine. Maybe I threw my Bible across the room in a rage. I'm not sure what kind of reaction those answers would elicit from the kind of person who would ask me that question, but luckily no one asks anymore.

When I was little, I was the kind of kid who prayed for forgiveness more times than I can remember for accidentally saying "oh my god." I feared for days that I would go to hell for taking the Lord's name in vain. These days, however, I'm more the person I described earlier. If you ask me what changed, I'd shrug but probably say something to the effect of 'I learned that God can take it.'

The summer before my senior year of college, I marathoned through this anime called *Tokyo Ghoul.* The story follows first-year college student Ken Kaneki who becomes a half-ghoul (a human-eating parallel species to humans) after receiving transplanted ghoul organs to save his life. When he wakes up, he discovers that he has odd new powers and, most disturbingly, that he has a hunger for human flesh. The only thing ghouls can safely digest is human flesh (oddly enough, they can also drink coffee). Most ghouls isolate themselves and become hunters. But some ghouls band together to try blending into the human world, committing to feed only on already dead bodies. These are the ghouls Kaneki finds himself with.

Shortly after his transformation, Kaneki finds himself out of control with his powers. Yomo, a ghoul who took him in, attempts to calm him. In his hunger-induced feeding frenzy, Kaneki lashes out at Yomo, who takes the brunt of his hysteria. Yomo tells Ken not to worry, to let it all out until he has calmed down enough to eat because he won't truly hurt him, a mature ghoul in control of their vast regenerative abilities. In that moment, Kaneki is able to release his suppressed ghoul and eventually calm down, eat, and get his powers under control.

I didn't realize it at the time, but I think this is reflective of one aspect of our relationship with God. In Christian subculture, we're so often taught to suppress and fight *against* our anger—a normal response to a variety of life experiences—similarly to how Kaneki suppressed his ghoul hunger and refused to eat. But eventually, everyone who continues to do this will snap, just like Kaneki's ghoul instincts finally took over when he had reached the point of starvation.

Just as Kaneki had been conditioned to believe he was evil for eating human flesh, even if he wasn't hurting anyone—I think many of us have been conditioned to believe that strong emotions, particularly anger directed towards the Divine, are evil—even if we aren't hurting anyone. So we stuff it down deeper and deeper until we eventually lose control.

The thing is, though—we forget that God is a lot more like Yomo than we like to think. We delude ourselves into thinking God will punish, ridicule, or ignore us when we're angry. Perhaps it's because that's how other people have responded to us in anger, but we don't realize that we won't truly hurt God, even when we're angry. They can take it.

And if we don't believe that, maybe we need to expand our view of who God is. Because if we truly believe God is who She says She is, we also need to believe God is bigger than our anger and pain ever could be; not in a dismissive way, but in a way that says, *'He can handle that uncontrolled grief, pain, loss, or anger in a way that others can't, even if we unleash it all on Him.'*

We also have to believe that maybe faith looks like believing God can take the force of all that power and emotion and that doing so is something They want to do out of love to help us make it through another day.

Sometimes, like Kaneki, we overestimate the power of our anger, our pain, whatever it may be; we become afraid that if we confront what's inside and let it out, no one will survive the aftermath. But the reality is that like in *Tokyo Ghoul*, God steps into the full force of the blast and embraces us, saying "I can take it." And sometimes, in order to truly heal and come to terms with things, we need to trust Her and believe that it's true.

God, help us learn new ways to cast our cares onto You. Help us to know and believe You can take what might feel like the worst of what we're holding back, and help us heal through our anger, our pain, and our loss.

This devotion was adapted from
"Everything Is Holy: Spiritual Truths from Anime"
by Jonah Venegas

A SPARK OF THE DIVINE WITHIN

ELIZABETH JEFFRIES

Then God said, "Let us make humanity in our image to resemble us so that they may take charge of the fish of the sea, the birds in the sky, the livestock, all the earth, and all the crawling things on earth."

Genesis 1:26 (CEB)

I grew up with a strong belief in God and a lot of encouragement to place my trust in Him. Perhaps like many evangelical Christians, I was taught about a God who resides in Heaven, far away from earth, who can only enter our world and our hearts because of the death of Jesus on the cross.

My God was far away, and even though this God was powerful and creative enough to be involved in my earthly life, He was only ever involved if He chose to reach down from His vantage point on high.

This God, I believed, was worthy of my full trust. Not only was He worthy, but trusting in this God was the only way that my life could be truly directed by Him. I believed in God's one and only plan for my life, and I believed my duty was to discover that plan. The only problem was that God's plan for my life felt as distant as God Himself. This all began to change when I noticed this brief passage in the creation poem at the beginning of Genesis. In this passage, when God decides to create mankind, He creates us in God's own image.

If I was made in the image of God, there must be something deep in me that recognizes and responds to goodness. There must be an inner spark of the Divine, somewhere within my deepest, truest self.

Make this your mantra today:
"I am the image of the Divine."

This devotion was adapted from
"Divine Direction"
by Elizabeth Jeffries

II · RECONSTRUCTION

Someone says "reconstruction," and I can't help but think of a broken hand with shattered bones that require much time and surgical precision to repair; and no matter how well the surgery goes, the hand is never the same again.

While a faith reconstruction is the act of putting back together one's deconstructed belief system, maybe it's better to describe the process as "selective choosing." Before, we may have guzzled down whatever theologies were placed before us by The Church. Reconstruction, this selective choosing, requires us to inspect and test the theologies that come our way. It is about rebuilding our faith around our new understanding about God and love—not dogma.

In this section, we are challenged to accept ourselves and others for who we are. With principles of social justice and solidarity at its core, reconstruction can give birth to a passionate love affair with Justice, Community, and Otherness. It all starts with the will to reconcile our faith with an un-boxed view of God.

We invite you in.

@nakedpastor

"Two Views"
DAVID HAYWARD

CHAPTER 5
Restoration

One of the best lessons I learned from my first adult relationship was how to have healthy fights with my partner. People in love will always have disagreements. It's normal. It's wise to acknowledge that there will be arguments. Messy ones, big ones, passive ones... but when we learn to argue with the intent to come to a resolution rather than to simply win, we invert it from a tool used for harm to a tool of growth.

Being a Christian is also being in a relationship—where disagreements and doubts are inevitable. But how can we learn to lean in to our doubts and use them as a tool to suss out the truth, to trust our intuitions, to discern what the correct next step is?

This section is all about repurposing the tools that have been used against us to work as a means of healing. Part of restoration is unlearning the dichotomies of good and bad, right and wrong until we are rid of those limiting binaries. Like stripping old paint from a door to expose and sand the wood underneath, it can be an arduous process. But it is also *freeing* and opens us up to countless new ways of accessing the Divine.

My prayer for you is that through restoration, you will welcome the rigorous changes until your smooth finish glows with a shiny new coat of paint.

We invite you in.

THE SPIRIT GIVES LIFE
MEL GARMAN

*The thief enters only to steal, kill, and destroy. I came so that they could
have life—indeed, so that they could live life to the fullest.*
John 10:10 (CEB)

The story doesn't end with death. After burial comes resurrection.

And soon, if we have not already, we shall rise. Against all adversity, I
believe we will. And the holes now in our hands? The scars on our side? The
pricks on our heads? They're evidence of a pain so deep we cannot forget—
but as C.S. Lewis said, there are far better things ahead than any we leave
behind. I dare to believe it.

Soon will come a day where we will no longer be burdened by the theological millstones that were tied around our necks, the political yokes that
weigh down our shoulders. We have conquered Death itself: the monstrous
belief system that people from our past indoctrinated us into. The rotten
ideological fruit that taught us to hate ourselves, hate others, hate the Earth—
we will proudly roll each of those stones away from the tomb they laid for
us. It will take work, of course. It might take therapy, medication, healthy
relationships, and other measures. But we will do it. We have to try, anyway.

And sure: a few will doubt us. They will doubt that we could have made
it this far or that we've found joy in our new lives and beliefs. But oh, how
many more will bear witness to our freedom! When we died, we took the
keys of liberation from Hell itself—the very real Hell they may have created
for us in their churches, their Christian schools, their ministries.

All of their schemes are now laid bare. We see how they engage in the
obsessive practice of calling evil "good" and calling good "evil." We uncover
their efforts and boldly proclaim: "No more!"

Unlike they told us, we never needed salvation from harmless hobbies, personal tastes, and natural human desires. Our gender expression, outfit choices, healthy relationships, and cultural practices were never of concern to God. If we've needed salvation from anything, it was from patriarchy, racism, queerphobia, purity culture, forced behavioral modification, mandatory ritualism, and authoritarian theology.

As 2 Corinthians 3:6 says, "the letter kills, but the Spirit gives life" (NRSV). We are free at last.

Scripture says that where the Spirit of the Lord is, there is freedom.
What methods or means of expressing the fullness of your identity do you find freeing?
It is there that you meet the Holy Spirit.

This devotion was adapted from
"Reconstruction as Resurrection"
by Mel Garman

YOUR HEALED SELF

REV. MIRIAM SAMUELSON-ROBERTS

> *I will restore your health,*
> *and I will heal your wounds,*
> *declares the Lord,*
> *because you were labeled an outcast,*
> *"Zion, the lost cause."*
>
> **Jeremiah 30:17 (CEB)**

Around the New Year, when I glance at magazines in my doctor's office or in grocery store aisles, I notice one prominent theme: new year, new you. The logical part of my brain that's into body positivity and smashing oppressive patriarchal ideals of what bodies should look like glances and looks away, but I'll sheepishly admit that there is some allure to being *new*.

I admit this sheepishly because it's literally the opposite of what I preach week after week as a pastor. I tell people: Look, you are fine exactly the way you are. You are valued, and you are loved. And because you know you are loved, you can go out and get to work in the world uplifting values, systems, and structures that help others know they are loved—all the while, dismantling what doesn't reflect that love. At the core of all of this is the fact that God loves you with no strings attached.

So even though that's what I preach and do ultimately believe, there are so few spaces that I actually get that message in my life. The messages I most often hear, or at least the ones I tend to hold onto, include: You are never going to be good enough, or busy enough, or efficient enough, or have it together enough (and by the way, here are some things you can buy to make those things magically happen).

There is a therapist in my community who asks people: "What does your healed self look like?" Not your new-and-improved self. Not your self who strives to be someone they aren't. But your *healed* self.

If you have one of those Bibles that has the titles of each story as you flip through the pages, pick any Gospel—especially Matthew, Mark, and Luke: the Synoptic Gospels that all tell similar stories—and look at the story titles. So many of them start with "Jesus Heals — ." This was one of the main things that Jesus's ministry was about. And you know what almost all these stories have in common? After the person was healed, they were reconnected with the community. Jesus heals people with leprosy because society wouldn't allow them to come near, and he wants people to be able to live in community together.

So often, allowing ourselves to be healed has ripple effects that extend into our relationships, our communities, and the world. If hurt people hurt people (as the saying goes), then surely healed people heal people. Healing isn't just a self-referential process. It always moves toward community, toward a more whole world.

So sit with my therapist friend's question: What does your healed self look like? Not a new self, not a better self, but a healed self. Take some time to live into that idea. Breathe into your body as it is, here and now, and connect with what healing feels like in your body and your soul. You are beautiful, and sacred, and loved exactly as you are. Let the healing power of that love flow over you, and in you, and around you. You are, and always will be, enough.

May you be able to imagine your healed self living and moving and breathing
in the world, and may you know the joy and groundedness of that healing,
here and now. May you be healed for the healing of the world.
Amen.

This devotion was adapted from
"New Year, Healed Me"
by Rev. Miriam Samuelson-Roberts

DIVINE ETERNAL PRESENCE
BRANDAN ROBERTSON

There was a Pharisee named Nicodemus, a Jewish leader. He came to Jesus at night
and said to him, "Rabbi, we know that you are a teacher who has come from God,
for no one could do these miraculous signs that you do unless God is with him."
Jesus answered, "I assure you, unless someone is born anew,
it's not possible to see God's kingdom."

John 3:1-3 (CEB)

When Jesus was speaking to the Jewish leader Nicodemus in John 3, he uttered the words that are popularly presented as the phrase "In order to enter the Kingdom of God, you must be born again."

These words have probably been quoted in just about every church around the world, but what exactly do they mean? I want to suggest that to be born again, or anew, has less to do with some magical transformation of our souls; rather, it is about the opening of our eyes to the enchantment of the world. Directly after Jesus says those words, he reiterates that "unless someone is born of water and the Spirit, it's not possible to enter God's kingdom." (John 3:5, CEB).

Jesus says you can see and enter the Kingdom of God right now. For Jesus, the Kingdom is our life and our world as God intends it to be. Jesus teaches that the ideal world already exists. Our abundant and whole life is available right now. The question is: do we see it?

The Proverb writer tells us to acknowledge God in all our ways (Proverbs 3:6). In other words, we must be aware and alerted to God's continual presence in every aspect of our lives. God is always present and is always at work in and around us; but most of the time, we are so distracted with anxiety or hustling to the next thing that we fail to stop, breathe, and perceive God's presence in our lives.

Even in our darkest moments, in our moments of failure or pain, we have access to the infinite presence of the Eternal Parent who extends love and wisdom to us whenever we need it. But we've got to renew our mind, slow down, and open our eyes to perceive this presence in our midst. God is with you, even right now as you read these words.

When you begin to perceive God in your day-to-day life, you may begin to live with more passion, purpose, and wonder—and these are ingredients for an extraordinary life.

This devotion was adapted from
"Perspective Shift"
by Brandan Robertson

RECONSTRUCTING EARTH

JASON KOON

Then the angel showed me the river of life-giving water, shining like crystal,
flowing from the throne of God and the Lamb through the middle of the city's main
street. On each side of the river is the tree of life, which produces twelve crops of fruit,
bearing its fruit each month. The tree's leaves are for the healing of the nations.
There will no longer be any curse. The throne of God and the Lamb will be in it, and
his servants will worship him. They will see his face, and his name will be on their
foreheads. Night will be no more. They won't need the light of a lamp or the light of
the sun, for the Lord God will shine on them, and they will rule forever and always.

Revelation 22:1-5 (CEB)

There are few times I feel more alive than when I'm running out in nature. The cool breeze blowing against my face and the smell of dirt and pine pitch filling my nostrils, as the endorphin rush of pushing through my initial bout with exhaustion propels me into energy reserves I never even knew I had. The roar of the waterfalls, the majesty of a mountain top, and the sacred quietness of the forest floor are medicine to me.

According to science, there is something to this. Few things have been able to combat my depression and anxiety in the way that exercise, fresh air, and sunshine can. My faith tells me it's because I was created for these things. Humanity was formed from the dirt and placed in a garden to live and work—indoors was our idea. Even when it comes to the afterlife, much of our religious imagery points toward a return to our earthly roots rather than an escape into the sky.

In Revelation 22, all the allusions to Eden are present in the new creation. Eastern Orthodox traditions pick up on this, imagining Paradise as an eternal garden or an incomparably beautiful cathedral. In Islam, the Qur'an's dominant image of the afterlife is also a garden that promises perfect peace to the faithful. Even in the Americas, centuries before any contact with Christianity or Islam, the Oglala Lakota saw the afterlife as a perfect nature preserve with unlimited hunting and an endless supply of game. There seems to be something universally human about our desire to one day return to the Paradise we are squandering.

So, what happens when we replace the ethereal picture of heaven with this earthy, organic vision of Paradise?

It means we are inseparably connected to the ground. This wasn't a difficult concept for our ancestors, who took their food directly from it. No wonder Genesis depicts God creating humanity from the ground. Where else would life come from? For us, however, modern society has put several layers between us and the Earth. It still is our source of life, but it seems much more indirect. In imagining eternity as the redemption of this ground we've taken for granted, our faith reminds us that we've always been connected to the rest of creation and promises that we always will be.

This promise fills the here-and-now with new purpose. My job is no longer just something I do to pass the time before being ushered into some detached ethereal spirit-plane; it is a spiritual practice. The same is true with household chores, yard work, and hobbies, which become sacred spaces where I can glimpse eternity and commune with the Divine.

How often do you recognize your unbreakable connection to the Earth?
What about modern life makes it hard to think this way?

This devotion was adapted from
"Deconstructing Heaven"
by Jason Koon

CHAPTER 6
Social Justice

Late 2017 when I started reaching out to authors to populate the shelves of Our Bible App with daily devotionals, I stumbled upon a phrase that gripped my heart: "From the pews to the protest." To this day, my mind becomes consumed with the phrase every time I am compelled into the streets—wielding a sign and chanting into the hot sun, "No justice, no peace!"

In my reconstruction, I learned that the pew is what propelled me to the protest.

Isn't that who Jesus was? One of the most memorable stories of Jesus at a temple involves him angrily flipping tables, making a mess of people's coins and inventory, wildly disrupting business. His worship was in the streets—empowering and sticking up for the marginalized, the disenfranchised.

Whether you leave your church pew altogether or find a way to incorporate protest and solidarity into your spiritual life as I have, I know that once you begin practicing your faith in a way that recognizes and rails against social injustice—you will never be able to unsee it.

We invite you in.

Relationship & Justice
Gena Thomas

The Lord of heavenly forces proclaims:
Make just and faithful decisions; show kindness and compassion to each other!
Don't oppress the widow, the orphan, the stranger, and the poor;
don't plan evil against each other!
Zechariah 7:9-10 (CEB)

What is justice? What are mercy and compassion? How are they connected?

The two Hebrew words found in the Old Testament for justice are *mishpat* and *tzedakah*. *Mishpat* means "giving others what they are due." *Tzedakah* means a *"life of right relationship."* So imagine I gave you a folder with a lifetime of information on 25-year-old Sam and another folder with the information about 25-year-old Chris. One of these 25-year-olds is supposed to receive a scholarship, and the other must go to jail for a crime they committed. You must decide who receives which outcome, but you are not allowed to read what's in the folders before your decision. What do you do?

There can be no justice in this scenario because there is no relationship. Without knowing anything about other human beings, without any relationship with them—we cannot begin to know what is properly due to them. When we distance ourselves immensely from others we disagree with, relationship has been taken away. (I am not referring to an abusive or toxic relationship here.)

Oftentimes, we no longer see the other as human as we see ourselves. We take away tzedakah. It's so easy to distance ourselves from others and pretend as though we are "doing justice" like Micah 6:8 calls us to, but the reality is that we cannot do justice without relationship.

Here's where love comes in. When we, without love, decide what another human being is due—we dehumanize that person. We cannot administer true justice without first recognizing the love that is due to others based on their divine imprint—the *Imago Dei*—which Genesis 1:26 so clearly bestowed upon every human being.

In today's ever-polarizing world, we are a people called to love others because God first loved us. We are a people called to administer true justice to the people on the other side of the other side of the computer screen, the political aisle, our country's border.

We cannot do justice if we are not in relationship with one another. And we cannot administer justice if we cannot first administer love.

God of Justice, Give us fresh knowledge of our own divine imprint.
Make us aware of the subtle ways we dehumanize each other and
give us the boldness to confess and to love.
May we experience justice as a reflection of your true character.
Amen.

This devotion was adapted from
"Love & Justice | Hand & Glove"
by Gena Thomas

SOCIAL JUSTICE AS WORSHIP

KATRINA ANNA MCINTOSH

Take away the noise of your songs;
I won't listen to the melody of your harps.
But let justice roll down like waters,
and righteousness like an ever-flowing stream.
Amos 5:23-24 (CEB)

Worship seems to be one of those incredible moments—those surreal experiences, when I am neither a captive of time nor space. Worship is a time when I am able to empty myself yet leave completely full. But my problem always lies in the aftermath. How do I carry over these surreal, epic moments into my everyday life?

When we move from seeing God as this untouchable mystical being to a very real person, friend, comforter, and everything in-between, worship moves from being a Levitical process to a force in every moment. To borrow a quote from my book *Letters to the Broken, Healing and Healed:* "To state [that] He is omnipresent and then limit His presence is a mathematical equation that results in nothingness." I believe that when we are able to grasp this revelation, we start becoming radical people of faith in constant conversation with God.

When this happens, worship is no longer dependent on emotional stimulations like musical arrangements or perfect scenery. Instead, it simply becomes a natural act. A permanent partnership. I liken this to close relationships. We can find comfort in one another during late night car rides, packed get-togethers, or just a random "hey, what's up" text. The moments are not limited. But they are all perfect in the ability to provide the exact sustenance needed for that time.

How do we then apply this to justice? Embracing the idea that God is in fact everywhere and that the process of worshipping God is an unlimited occurrence—why can't we express that act of worship when seeking out justice? Amos 5:24 tells us to "let justice roll down like waters" (CEB). This, to me, is a beautiful visual showing the impact that justice should make. It begins as a stream springing forth, sometimes in an unlikely situation. It perseveres downhill, joins other immaculate forces, and develops into a bed of resources. A bed of impact. A bed that provides nourishment for parched mouths and homes for fauna.

We are these rivers. We are these justice carriers. We are these powerful entities who create unexpected paths. We are many rivers, all meeting in this endless ocean of power and hope. This is what justice brings. And this is what worship does.

In worship, particularly through the act of social justice work, advocates can empty themselves and still be utterly filled. It is a place where the most important commandment is carried out: complete and utter adoration for God occurs with all heart, soul, mind, and strength; and love for another is expressed with the same adoration as the love for self.

In the moment when an advocate desires the same justice to be given to another that is afforded to them, or they seek to fight for the needs of marginalized communities—this, to me, is worship. Selfless, sacrificial worship.

This devotion was adapted from
"Advocacy & Social Justice"
by Katrina Anna McIntosh

INTRAPERSONAL
JUSTICE WORK
MADISON CHAU

Why do you see the splinter in your brother's or sister's eye but don't notice the log in your own eye? How can you say to your brother or sister, 'Brother, Sister, let me take the splinter out of your eye,' when you don't see the log in your own eye?
You deceive yourselves! First take the log out of your eye, and then you will see clearly to take the splinter out of your brother's or sister's eye.

Luke 6:41-42 (CEB)

You know what's way easier than engaging in difficult conversations about your own biases and participation in unjust systems? Calling other people out on theirs. I'm incredibly guilty of this. How much easier is it to send out a quick Tweet about the shortcomings we see in other people's activism? There's very little risk, and it makes us look good for noticing injustice.

We live in a world where the scale has historically been tipped in favor of certain groups over others, and living in that world means certain biases have been bred within us from birth. Even the most seasoned activists are not immune to bias. Every single one of us has a responsibility to work through them internally. It's important to do justice work, but it's just as important to continually check ourselves for our own logs in our eyes. Attending a protest against police brutality, for example, means little if we call the police on our Black neighbor the next day for playing music too loud.

Justice work is both systemic and intrapersonal; we will never fully achieve one without the other.

When we commit ourselves to justice work, we must commit to starting that work in our own hearts, starting with the log in our own eye.

This devotion was adapted from
"On Hypocrisy"
by Madison Chau

COMMUNITY & ADVOCACY
REV. CLAIRE BROWN

Jesus was telling them a parable about their need to pray continuously and not to be discouraged. He said, "In a certain city there was a judge who neither feared God nor respected people. In that city there was a widow who kept coming to him, asking, 'Give me justice in this case against my adversary.'
For a while he refused but finally said to himself, I don't fear God or respect people, but I will give this widow justice because she keeps bothering me. Otherwise, there will be no end to her coming here and embarrassing me." The Lord said, "Listen to what the unjust judge says. Won't God provide justice to his chosen people who cry out to him day and night? Will he be slow to help them? I tell you, he will give them justice quickly. But when the Human One comes, will he find faithfulness on earth?"

Luke 18:1-8 (CEB)

This parable can be read as a paradigm for social change and community relations. When individuals or communities need to bring about a change of power relations, continuing to protest or petition in adversity is often effective over time—a key to successful community organizing and sustainable solutions. The introduction presents the story as a model for persistence in personal prayer.

A translation of the original Greek reveals that the widow's impact on the judge could be a potentially violent one, which can be understood as giving the judge a "black eye," according to AJ Levine's work on this text. The judge must be projecting this violent nature on her, right? Resistance tactics that inconvenience or impede smoothly functioning power structures are often decried as violent and unreasonable, taking things too far. Her resistance succeeds in spite of his position and authority, in spite of his false rhetoric that undermines her work.

Or does it? The stories of Jesus are full of rich detail, but this parable is silent about some important questions. What is she seeking justice for? Is her complaint valid? Is it possible that the tactics and threats are a concern? The only inner monologue is the concern of the judge, her opponent; I have to at least entertain the idea of his side of the story.

Advocacy and organizing, like any human endeavor, is susceptible to vilifying and valorizing along the lines of social location in ways that refuse this ambiguity. What this parable lacks (whether it's read for prayer or advocacy) is community presence and accountability. When we find ourselves in the widow's position, we need others' voices along with our own—to strengthen and expedite our petition, to give us the balanced perspective of moral accountability to a larger community vision.

Jesus sent disciples out in pairs and groups to do world changing work. Don't neglect the community that holds you up and calls you to live and love more deeply.

This devotion was adapted from
"Ambiguous Advocacy: Fighting for Ourselves"
by Rev. Claire Brown

THE EARTH IS HURTING
REV. EJ MCGAUGHY

I've heard many climate change activists and theologians claim that the Earth is our great equalizer, that it's literally our common ground. And while I don't debate the planet's absolute essentiality for all of us is because, according to the Bible, we are creatures of the dust—literally formed by and from the land—therefore not materially separate from the Earth. I don't think it's honest to claim that ecological degradation, or the impact of "natural" disasters, impacts all communities in the same way with the same severity.

> Disabled people are more vulnerable.
>
> People of color are more vulnerable.
>
> Poor people are more vulnerable.
>
> Young children are more vulnerable.
>
> The elderly are more vulnerable.
>
> Immigrants are more vulnerable.
>
> Refugees are more vulnerable.

Not because of who these groups are, essentially, but because of how social systems of oppression render certain people more vulnerable to disaster. This is what systems of oppression do. And it hurts us all over.

Legendary civil rights activist and theologian Ruby Sales once did an interview with Krista Tippet for the *On Being* podcast. The episode's title was "Where Does It Hurt?"

Where does it hurt? This isn't just a question, she told us. It's a way of orienting to the world. *Where Does it Hurt?*

Any of us trained in work like therapy, social work, or pastoral care knows what a powerful question this can be. Not, *does* it hurt—but *where*. It's a way of orienting to the world that takes suffering seriously. To draw on Sales' words, "it unleashes a territory" that gets "to the source of the pain."

So today, in light of the global disasters in our midst, I want us to take up the question intentionally. If we were to take theologian Sally McFague seriously and render our Earth the "Body of God," and ask it *Where does it hurt?* — how might the Earth reply today? Right now?

And as we face our Earth, the Body of God, hurting all over today, we cannot avoid asking a follow-up question: Why does it hurt?

This devotion was adapted from
"Where Does It Hurt?"
by Rev. EJ McGaughy

HOLY DEFIANCE
JASMIN FIGUEROA

The king of Egypt spoke to two Hebrew midwives named Shiphrah and Puah:
"When you are helping the Hebrew women give birth and you see the baby being born,
if it's a boy, kill him. But if it's a girl, you can let her live." Now the two midwives
respected God so they didn't obey the Egyptian king's order. Instead, they let the baby
boys live. So the king of Egypt called the two midwives and said to them,
"Why are you doing this? Why are you letting the baby boys live?"
Exodus 1:15-18 (CEB)

This Bible passage opens in the beginning of the book of Exodus. In the story, the Israelite people had been living and prospering in Egypt for a generation. Thanks to the warm relationship between their ancestor Joseph and Egyptian leaders, both communities coexisted in peace. That is, until a new pharaoh came into power.

This new leader neither knew Joseph's legacy, nor did he respect Joseph's descendants. Instead, he saw them as a burden and a threat that needed to be vanquished; so began their oppression. He began by forcing them into manual labor and added increasingly ruthless policies that ensured they would suffer greatly.

And yet, the story tells us that the Israelites survived the conditions that the Egyptians wrought upon them, and their numbers continued to increase. The enraged pharaoh retaliated by ordering the Hebrew midwives to put every male child they helped bring into the world to death. But the midwives—two women named Shiprah and Puah—refused to carry out these orders.

Verse 17 says that "[they] feared God; they did not do as the king of Egypt commanded them, but they let the boys live." God saw this and blessed the midwives and the Israelites, increasing their numbers more and more.

While I've always been able to appreciate the risk that Shiprah and Puah took to defy Pharaoh's orders, this story is hitting closer to home for me these days. I cannot help but read this story and see parallels between the pharaoh's cruelty towards the Israelite people and the United States's cruelty towards immigrant and refugee populations who are seeking shelter and opportunity in this country.

Because our understanding of the current immigration crisis cannot be complete without acknowledging the U.S.'s complicity in destabilizing the countries surrounding us, it is even more frustrating to note that we continue to draw boundaries around these communities through shifting borders, exclusionary policies, walls, detention centers, and xenophobic attitudes.

As story after story breaks concerning politicians' inflammatory rhetoric, hate crimes throughout the country, or inhumane conditions in modern-day concentration camps, it is clear that—in the words of The Atlantic columnist Adam Serwer—"the cruelty is the point."

One can feel helpless in the face of such inhumanity, particularly when moments like these reveal the seemingly impenetrable boundary between those in power and those who are most vulnerable within our society.

The part of me that is familiar with the effects of vicarious trauma cannot help but imagine what it must have been like for Shiprah and Puah to have been ordered to directly contribute to the suffering of their communities.

This, too, was an act of cruelty on behalf of the pharaoh—to make them complicit in their own dehumanization and to conscript them into murdering their own people. And yet, the story says that they "feared God" and refused to take part in the deaths of their people and their own humanity.

When I imagine what it must have been like for these women to make that decision, I'm sure that it wasn't as easy as the story portrays it to be. While it simply says that she did not do as Pharaoh asked, I envision all of the turmoil that must have occurred surrounding that decision. After all, they were already known by the Pharaoh, so surely their lives were also at risk if their defiance was discovered.

I imagine their serious conversations as Shiprah and Puah contemplated the danger before them. I picture them pushing through waves of nausea deep in their gut, as they attempted to move forward as normally as possible, continuing to help mothers through the birthing process and advise them on how to hide themselves and their babies afterwards.

I cannot help but contemplate the inner strength and conviction that led them to make this decision. While the story is clear that they "feared God," I imagine that these words fall short of all of the emotions they experienced.

Not only must they have feared God, but I also imagine that this fear was buttressed by a deep love for their community. They loved their people too much to let Pharaoh's death-dealing boundaries dictate their decisions. They loved the community too much to let fear for their own lives stop them from doing what was right in that moment. They loved their community too much to prohibit themselves from feeling their righteous anger and to keep them from languishing in complacency.

Instead, they decided to counter Pharaoh's mandate with a boundary of their own: No. They would not follow Pharaoh's orders, and no, they would not remain neutral in the face of cruelty and danger. No, they would not be complicit in the deaths of their children.

It was their own love that propelled them to disregard Pharaoh's boundaries, and counter with some of their own. They would not give into the fear that would have them follow Pharaoh's orders, but would draw deeply from the love of their community to give them the strength that they needed to resist and survive.

Stories like this, unfortunately, are not new. Boundaries that exclude and dehumanize people exist, and power dynamics that would keep us complacent are powerfully influential. As people who exist in this world and lament the injustices that surround us, what can we possibly do?

I want to invite us to consider the example of Shiprah and Puah, two women who used whatever resources they could for the sake of their communities.

I want to invite us to consider the ways that love for one another can motivate us to push beyond the boundaries that would seek to destroy us, and instead, show us another way.

This devotion was adapted from
"Learning Boundaries"
by Jasmin Figueroa

CHAPTER 7
Disability Theology

Without much realizing it, Christianity has built a faith tradition steeped heavily in ableism. How often in our sermons and faith sharing groups do we encounter language equating disability with sin, anecdotes about miraculous healings awarded to those with "enough" faith, or unwelcome prayer attempts to heal what was never an illness to begin with? How inaccessible to disabled people are our church buildings, worship experiences, or the myriad other community events and resources?

This chapter shares glimpses into the spiritual worldview of authors who encounter the Divine through the lenses of their disabilities, chronic illnesses, and chronic pain. As you engage with the lessons and reflections shared in this chapter, remember that the face of God is made more whole when we include disabled people in our Divine imagination.

We invite you in.

UNITY THROUGH
CELEBRATING DIFFERENCES
STEPHANIE TAIT

Certainly the body isn't one part but many. If the foot says, "I'm not part of the body because I'm not a hand," does that mean it's not part of the body? If the ear says, "I'm not part of the body because I'm not an eye," does that mean it's not part of the body? If the whole body were an eye, what would happen to the hearing? And if the whole body were an ear, what would happen to the sense of smell? But as it is, God has placed each one of the parts in the body just like he wanted. If all were one and the same body part, what would happen to the body? But as it is, there are many parts but one body. So the eye can't say to the hand, "I don't need you," or in turn, the head can't say to the feet, "I don't need you." Instead, the parts of the body that people think are the weakest are the most necessary. The parts of the body that we think are less honorable are the ones we honor the most. The private parts of our body that aren't presentable are the ones that are given the most dignity. The parts of our body that are presentable don't need this. But God has put the body together, giving greater honor to the part with less honor so that there won't be division in the body and so the parts might have mutual concern for each other. If one part suffers, all the parts suffer with it; if one part gets the glory, all the parts celebrate with it. You are the body of Christ and parts of each other.

1 Corinthians 12:14-27 (CEB)

Many people seem to be uncomfortable with the term "disabled." There are countless euphemisms employed in its place, from "differently-abled," to "special needs," to "handi-capable." Proponents of these alternative terms claim they're more positive and thereby more respectful. But in reality? This reluctance to use the word "disabled" is rooted in an ableist perspective that doesn't fully celebrate the image of God in disabled bodies. In insisting that calling someone disabled may be "offensive," we reveal that we see disability itself as undesirable, suggesting that it could be insulting to be associated with that label. We assume that differences exist in a hierarchy where acknowledging someone as disabled is identifying them as "less than" or "worse."

Paul addressed this very sort of ableism and hierarchical thinking in his letter to the church in Corinth. There are some key truths in Paul's message that can help reshape not only the way we think about disabled people, but how we treat them as well.

First, Paul doesn't ask us to focus on what we have in common. In a letter urging unity in the church, Paul intentionally speaks to what makes us each different as the key. He writes, "If the whole body were an eye, what would happen to the hearing? And if the whole body were an ear, what would happen to the sense of smell?" (v. 17) His message here is clear: Unity is not uniformity. Unity is not homogeneity. And unity is not leaving our differences at the door and trying to focus only on the things we share in common. Our diversity is a key component of God's design, and any attempt to downplay those differences leaves us unable to be the church of God's design.

Second, the upside-down economics of God's Kingdom brings glory to the things usually considered undesirable. Paul speaks directly to this, saying, "Instead, the parts of the body that people think are the weakest are the most necessary. The parts of the body that we think are less honorable are the ones we honor the most" (vv. 22-23). There is simply no place for ableism in the body of Christ. Disabled and chronically ill people have a wealth of wisdom and perspective to share, and it's vital to the health of the Church that we honor their essential roles in the body.

Third, tolerance is simply not good enough when it comes to the body of Christ. We are not called to tolerate our differences, but to celebrate them. We are not called to patronize or tokenize the disabled people in our midst, but to honor them as important leaders and teachers which the body of Christ depends on to be healthy and whole. We should be celebrating and cherishing the disabled people in our midst so well, that it becomes impossible to imagine how the word "disabled" could have ever been seen negatively in any way.

Finally, Paul leaves us with a vision of a fully-flourishing body of Christ that thrives in its diversity, noting that it's specifically through honoring the weak that we tear down the divisions between us. "But God has put the body together, giving greater honor to the part with less honor so that there won't be division in the body and so the parts might have mutual concern for each other. If one part suffers, all the parts suffer with it; if one part gets the glory, all the parts celebrate with it. You are the body of Christ and parts of each other" (vv. 25-27).

It is only when we honor disabled identity instead of seeking to whitewash our differences that we can become a healthier and more unified body of Christ, belonging wholly to each other.

If you are abled, here is a prayer for you:

Lord, show me the places I have unrecognized ableism in my words, in my theology, and in my behavior towards people who are disabled or chronically ill. Help me to better honor disabled identity, and show me ways that I can elevate disabled voices to lead us from their unique wisdom.

If you are disabled, here is a prayer for you:

Lord, show me the places I may have internalized ableism. Teach me greater love and acceptance for my disabled self. Empower me to teach and lead from the unique wisdom that comes from disability. May Your glory be most evident in my weakness.

This devotion was adapted from
"Disability Theology Is for Everyone
by Stephanie Tait

DISABILITY IS NOT
A PUNISHMENT
STEPHANIE TAIT

As Jesus walked along, he saw a man who was blind from birth. Jesus' disciples asked,
"Rabbi, who sinned so that he was born blind, this man or his parents?"
Jesus answered, "Neither he nor his parents. This happened so that God's mighty
works might be displayed in him.
John 9:1-3 (CEB)

It was almost 20 years ago when I first started to get sick. I went from a vibrant and exuberant teenage girl with a blossoming dance career on the horizon, to an unexplained patchwork of crushing fatigue, chronic pain, and life-altering neurological issues. Doctors were baffled as to what could be wrong with me, and every test came back with no discernible explanation for my steady decline. Each year that passed would bring a host of new symptoms, but rarely any answers.

In my desperation to get better, I turned to my faith. One question began to plague me above the rest: *Could God be trying to teach me a lesson, or perhaps be punishing me for some sort of hidden sin issue I just wasn't recognizing?*

I've heard versions of this same fear expressed again and again in the disability and chronic illness community: Is God doing this to me? Did I bring this on myself somehow? Would He heal me if I could just figure out what it is that He wants me to confess, or what it is that He wants me to change?

We can see in John 9 that Jesus's disciples had bought into this same narrative of shame and blame, questioning who was "at fault" for the disability of the man before them: "Rabbi, who sinned so that he was born blind," they asked him, "this man or his parents?" (v. 2)

For them, it wasn't an issue of whether this blindness was a punishment for sin, but simply a debate over whose sin was to blame. But Jesus responds with two key truths that point us to a very different view of disability and chronic illness.

First, He rejects the blame game. "Neither he nor his parents," Jesus responds (v. 3). Disability isn't a punishment for anyone's sin. Trying to assign blame for why someone is disabled or chronically ill isn't just a pointless endeavor; it's a rejection of the freedom from shame that Jesus offers us. Romans 8:1 tells us: "So now there isn't any condemnation for those who are in Christ Jesus" (CEB). Shame and blame are never of Christ, so we can reject any theology that tries to assign us that burden.

Second, He points to disability as a mark of God's glory, rather than His anger: "This happened so that God's mighty works might be displayed in him.," Christ declares (v. 3). Not only does He reject the notion that disability is a punishment, He also goes even further by holding up disability as an extended display of God's image and power.

It may seem almost nonsensical to us by today's cultural standards, and the disciples would have been equally confused by how God's glory could be displayed in the form of weakness and lack. And yet, we can read this same sentiment echoed again in the words of Paul from his letter to the Corinthians (2 Corinthians 12:9-10).

Ultimately, when it comes to disability and chronic illness, trying to search for a reason "why" these things happen can often prove frustratingly fruitless. But there are two things we can know for sure. One: disability is not a punishment for sin because in Christ, we find freedom from the blame game. And two: God's glorious image is on full display in disabled bodies. What a weighty gift to be entrusted to display those key facets of His image to a watching world.

If you are disabled, here is a prayer for you:
Lord, free me from the bondage of misplaced shame and blame.
Help me to see myself through Your eyes, so that I can fully recognize Your
glorious image in my disabled body.

If you are abled, here is a prayer for you:

Lord, help me identify any false blame I may be placing on those who are sick or disabled. Grant me eyes to see your power on glorious display in the bodies and lives of those who are disabled or chronically ill.

This devotion was adapted from
"Disability Theology Is for Everyone"
by Stephanie Tait

GOD'S INTENTIONALLY DIVERSE DESIGN
STEPHANIE TAIT

*But Moses said to the Lord, "My Lord, I've never been able to speak well,
not yesterday, not the day before, and certainly not now since you've been talking to
your servant. I have a slow mouth and a thick tongue."
Then the Lord said to him, "Who gives people the ability to speak?
Who's responsible for making them unable to speak or hard of hearing,
sighted or blind? Isn't it I, the Lord?*
Exodus 4:10-11 (CEB)

A woman attempted to comfort me one morning when my autistic son was having a difficult time at church. She placed her hand on my shoulder and said that she'd be "praying for his healing from autism." Before I could compose myself to respond, she added, "And take heart in the promise that there will be no more autism in heaven!"

She turned to head off in the other direction, and I immediately lowered myself to crouch at eye level with my son. I placed a hand on each side of his face and said, "You don't need to be healed of autism, because autism isn't a disease. God made you exactly the way He intended to, and I wouldn't dream of telling God he made a mistake. Of course there will be autism in heaven. If there wasn't any autism, there wouldn't be any autistic people there. That's not a heaven worth having."

Looking at God's conversation with Moses in Exodus, we see Him taking intentional responsibility for a number of disabilities. "Who's responsible for making them unable to speak or hard of hearing, sighted or blind? Isn't it I, the Lord?" (v. 11)

Now, should we read this verse to mean that God personally causes every illness, injury, or disability in this world? I don't believe so, no. That would contradict so much of what we see of God throughout the rest of s, and what we know of His heart for His creation. God is not somewhere sitting on a throne sending cancer, paralyzing car accidents, or brutal assaults. And yet, we are left with a clear depiction here of God taking responsibility for a number of disabilities as part of His perfect design. So what does that mean?

First, it's an important reminder to those who are abled that you should never assume someone's disability is a tragedy, a burden, or a mistake. Experiences of disabled identity are deeply varied, as well as deeply personal. Before offering someone healing prayer, it's essential to listen to their perspectives and ensure that you're respecting both their personhood and their consent. For many disabled people, their disability is not something they feel is separable from the rest of their identity. (This is especially true for much of the autism community, which is why most autistic adults prefer the term "autistic" over "person with autism.") In those cases, lamenting someone's disability is akin to lamenting that they exist at all, and this is deeply dehumanizing.

Second, consider the ways that the challenges related to many disabilities are caused by ableism and not by the disability itself. If people of different neurotypes or physical ability had their accessibility needs met, and those systemic barriers to inclusion were removed, how would that change our view of that disability?

Picture for a moment, your own ideas of heaven. How do you picture God will erase the communication barriers that can divide hearing and verbal people from people who are deaf/hard of hearing or nonverbal, for example? You may imagine that the deaf will be made to hear and the nonverbal will gain their speech. While that's certainly one possibility, it also assumes that abled people are the "norm" and that disabled people are the variant that will be "fixed." What if instead of erasing disabilities, the perfection of Heaven comes in erasing the barriers themselves? Perhaps, instead, it is the hearing who will gain the ability to understand sign language, and the verbal who will gain the ability to understand the many ways that nonverbal people communicate.

We serve a big, multidimensional God. It takes a diverse array of races, genders, personalities, neurotypes, sexual orientations, and abilities to fully reflect God's glorious image. In our limited human capacity, we can each contain just a piece of God's reflection, and it is only through His intentionally diverse design that we can see the complex tapestry of the *Imago Dei*.

If you are abled, here is a prayer for you:

Lord, help me to identify the ways my ableism may be discounting the beauty of your diverse design. Teach me to see people with disabilities as essential pieces to revealing the full glory of your image in us.

If you are disabled, here is a prayer for you:

Lord, empower me to boldly reflect the unique pieces of your image that you've entrusted me to carry. Give me the wisdom to recognize the lies of ableism and the strength to advocate for my inherent value and immutable worth.

This devotion was adapted from
"Disability Theology Is for Everyone"
by Stephanie Tait

AUTISTIC PRAYER
CARALYNN HAMPSON

In the same way, the Spirit comes to help our weakness. We don't know what we
should pray, but the Spirit himself pleads our case with unexpressed groans.
The one who searches hearts knows how the Spirit thinks, because he pleads for the
saints, consistent with God's will.
Romans 8:26-27 (CEB)

Autism isn't mentioned in the Bible. Obviously, the Diagnostic Standard
Manual (DSM) did not exist back then. However, autistic people are present
today; we sing and move with life that is glorious and wonderful. We process
information differently and view life from varying angles. We love with
passion and know the true definition of patience.

Prayer is beyond spoken language, beyond written language, beyond body
language, but it is still understood by God. When we are too weary to speak,
our God hears our prayers. When we are too overwhelmed to process our
surroundings, our God hears our prayers. When we are too excited to express
our ideas, our God hears our prayers. When we lack words to describe our
feelings, our God hears our prayers. When we can only whisper our needs,
our God hears our prayers. Our God hears our prayers.

Speech delays and language processing issues are common among autistic folk. Self-expression can be difficult. It is important to remember that
even when we struggle to express our worries and hopes, that God hears our
prayers. God receives our prayers even when we make no sound. As stated
in Matthew 6:8, God knows what we need before we ask.

Even without language, our God still knows our concerns, joys, and
desires. God hears us without language. The Holy Spirit is still guiding us even

when our brains seem to fail us. The Holy Spirit knows our prayers and does not require language for those prayers to be heard.

Prayer is where you are free to be yourself in all your createdness. In prayer, your full identity can be present. In prayer, you are a child of God. Neurodivergence does not exclude anyone from the peace that prayer can bring. The Holy Spirit is a mighty interpreter who knows our prayers when we cannot speak. The Holy Spirit is a strong guide who can help us understand the full love that God our Creator and Heavenly Parent has for us. The Holy Spirit is a force that can transform the prayers we have and instigate peace.

Prayer is a precursor to peace. There is no particular method of prayer that is superior to another, and peace is not exclusive to certain types of prayer. Praying as yourself in grunts, songs, speech, movement, whispers—however you feel comfortable—is important for knowing peace. Know that you were created by an awesome God and that your method of prayer is received by your creator.

Not all rules in society are useful, and many can mislead us to not know the full love of God. No matter how you exist, you are loved. Whether or not you perform the sign of the cross after each prayer, keep your eyes open, avoid eye contact, know the right words to say, or pray while kneeling—your prayer is heard. Your prayer is heard even when you do not use words or language. Our God hears our prayers.

May we be reminded that prayer does not need to be of an earthly language.
Amen.

This devotion was adapted from
"Autistic Prayer"
by Caralynn Hampson

THE POWER OF SHOULD
JASON KOON

"My grace is enough for you, because power is made perfect in weakness."
2 Corinthians 12:9 (CEB)

"Should" is a powerful and often misused word. It can be used appropriately to correct or to teach, but more often, it is wielded to wound and shame—to make people feel less than. Tragically, many have been led to believe that God is primarily in the business of "shoulds"— causing us to falsely attribute our own impossibly high, self-inflicted expectations to God instead of ourselves.

Most people in my life already know that I am in the early stages of a chronic illness—a rare form of Muscular Dystrophy. My particular condition—Myotonic Dystrophy—is not exactly the typical picture of Muscular Dystrophy that you might have in your head. For example, it works from the outside in—affecting my extremities more profoundly at first, before slowly moving in towards my core. This makes for some unusual challenges.

I work at the post office, and while you'd think it would be the fifty-pound packages that give me trouble, they're usually not a problem. It's actually the Sharpies I use to mark my parcels; my fingers don't have the strength to pinch off the marker's cap. A few weeks ago, I spread about two-dozen fifty-pound bags of gravel in a large flower bed in front of our house—no big deal. When I took a break, however, I couldn't open my bag of chips without going into the house for a pair of scissors.

Asking for help when I feel like I should be able to do something is humbling. My abilities are all over the place, but I'm not the only one with this problem. All of our capabilities are all over the place. Maybe it's more noticeable for me right now, but you too are a complex swirling blend of greatness and ineptitude.

I know a man who can barely hack his way through a book that I could skim in an hour or two, but he has more wisdom about life and faith than anyone else I've ever met. He's like that guy in the gym with massive arms, but legs so skinny we sometimes wonder how they hold him up. We're all like that guy in one way or another. We feel like we should be able to do better, but we don't know how.

As I said, "should" is a powerful word—so powerful I once cranked on a water bottle, trying to wrestle the cap off until my fingers bled because I "should" have been able to. Fortunately, the Apostle Paul offers an antidote to our "shoulds" in 2 Corinthians. According to Paul, God says to us: "My grace is enough for you, because power is made perfect in weakness" (2 Cor. 12:9, CEB). In other words, you are weak, just like I am; you have a condition not that different from mine. We are all fallen creatures—weird and broken—living in a weird and broken world. We are capable of incredible genius and profound stupidity, of inspiring altruism and horrific atrocity.

Through the centuries, many Christians have allowed this uncomfortable reality to crush them under the weight of self-inflicted expectations. Instead of falling victim to this way of thinking, however, I can empower this truth to liberate me from them.

God's grace speaks to me, even amid my brokenness. It embraces me exactly as I am, shouting down my "shoulds," melting them away, outing them as little more than cultural mirages. It liberates me to embrace myself, and it empowers me to extend that same embrace to others.

No matter who you are or where you're from, no matter what you've done—I can embrace you because I know there aren't nearly as many "shoulds" in this world as I've been led to believe there are.

Think about some of the self-inflicted expectations you have laid upon yourself. Thank God that God has embraced you exactly as you are and pray that God would help you to embrace yourself in the same way.

This devotion was adapted from
"The Power of Should"
by Jason Koon

LOOK FOR THE HELPERS

REV. BAILEY BRAWNER

Since there is one loaf of bread, we who are many are one body,
because we all share the one loaf of bread.

1 Corinthians 10:17 (CEB)

I have a lot of trouble asking for help. I like having it all together, and having chronic pain has always meant that I needed to have it all together even more since I already felt like a mess. I didn't want to acknowledge that there was something about me that needed help, even though I knew it to be true. Even something as silly as someone holding a door open for me felt like a signal broadcasting to the universe that I was incapable of doing it myself. Receiving help felt akin to weakness to me because in many ways, I already felt helpless.

I hold a lot of pride in what I can accomplish, but when my body began to turn on itself, physically altering how I was able to live, the routines and systems I created for myself no longer worked. When I moved from rural Alaska to San Diego, I had a pallet of my belongings shipped to me, and I went with Oakley to go pick up the goods. I pulled into the warehouse, and a guy drove up with all my stuff: bike, bookshelf, and boxes. He put it down and must have noticed the 'how will I get all this in my car?' look in my eyes, paired with my stubbornness and sheer willpower to persevere.

He asked me, "So, you got it from here?" I told him, "If you're offering to help, I will gladly accept." And I did. He basically loaded all of it into my Jeep as I kept a busy puppy from getting in his way, telling him where to put what and how much further he could push stuff forward. I drove home with no more aches and pains than when I started, and I know it also probably made his day to be able to make my life a little easier.

My friend Erynne DeVore, who works in children and family ministry at my home church, once preached an incredible sermon about how we are created to be in community, to thrive alongside one another, and how sometimes that means we need to ask for help: "As much as we were made to need each other, we were made to carry each other too."

She went on to talk about all the things that wouldn't have happened if she didn't both ask for and accept help from those around her. Even if everything had gotten done, even if she could have handled it all herself, she would have missed opportunities to connect, to feel loved, to strengthen relationships. Sometimes, people want to help, and we can make their day by saying yes.

We are all just trying to do our best to get by. It doesn't matter how good you have it—life is tough. We all worry about money and time and relationships, and perhaps that is the simplest proof that we are not alone. The body of Christ functions together, not separately, and that is good news. We need each other—to live, to love, to carry one another, and to be carried.

May you offer yourselves the freedom to say "yes" to the help around you. May you look beyond the pride and stubbornness and independence that has been ingrained in you. And may you know that asking for help does not make you helpless or a nuisance—it makes you brave.

This devotion was adapted from
"Let's Get Visible: Chronic Pain, Invisible Illness, and the Kindom of God"
by Bailey Brawner

CHAPTER 8
Love

"Treat yo'self" was a hilarious (and iconic) bit from the show *Parks and Recreation*, but something about the phrase really embedded itself into our culture. It pushed against a damning social construct that glorified a never-ending *hustle* and *grind* mentality that does not give adequate space for rest or pleasure. "Treat yo'self" told us, "It's okay to make yourself happy too," and we clung to it.

We live in an age of self-care, self-help, iClouds, iPhones—all formulated around individual enlightenment and enjoyment. We must recognize that movements like these don't just pop up out of thin air. There had to have been a cultural deficit, a global yearning to be loved in a way that was unreachable before.

Let's tune in to this self-care movement for a moment—because if we can learn to love ourselves better, it just makes sense that we would in turn learn how to love our neighbors better too.

It is here where we learn the breadth of our own heart's capabilities: to love ourselves beyond measure, deeply and unapologetically. And we learn to serve others in a way that requires us to improve our own dispositions.

We invite you in.

LOVE IS NOT PRODUCTION
JAMEELAH JONES

Love is patient, love is kind, it isn't jealous, it doesn't brag, it isn't arrogant,
it isn't rude, it doesn't seek its own advantage, it isn't irritable, it doesn't keep a record
of complaints, it isn't happy with injustice, but it is happy with the truth. Love puts
up with all things, trusts in all things, hopes for all things, endures all things.
Love never fails. As for prophecies, they will be brought to an end. As for tongues,
they will stop. As for knowledge, it will be brought to an end.
1 Corinthians 13:4-8 (CEB)

1 Corinthians 4-8 was drilled into my memory as a young Christian—as a roadmap for what to look for in a potential husband. Despite the incomplete ways this passage was taught to me, I always noticed that it didn't frame love as "work." I never felt that this passage wanted love to equate to labor, so I've always been confused by clichés like "friendship is hard work."

It's so easy to get caught up in motivational hot takes about love, like "Only maintain the relationships that add value to your life." This kind of advice on love can be a decent start to drawing boundaries, but connecting love to production is deep conditioning that discriminates based on capital and ability.

I have been diagnosed with severe adult attention deficit disorder (AADD). I forget things. Everything in my mind leaves as quickly as it comes, and there isn't a whole lot I can do about it. There is treatment for my ADD-related symptoms—except the forgetting. My medications can help with the present and the future, but not the past. And the second I do or think something, it becomes the past.

This means I have to consider a definition of love that does not center how capable I am of producing. There are times when I am incapable of producing a desired result for myself or others. This does not mean I am not worthy of love from God, myself, or others. I have to form a community that applies this definition of love to our relationships.

Additionally, I do not need a person to first produce for me before I can love them as God loves. I can, and should, develop love and empathy for people who do nothing to benefit me. This is not to say that we shouldn't set expectations within our relationships. Rather, we should question the kinds of expectations we set, especially any that feed into the idea that love is about someone's ability to produce for you.

God, help me see your love in all things and people. Help me see places where this world equates love to production. Give me the strength to be a counterbalance to definitions of love that focus on capitalist notions of work and labor.

This devotion was adapted from
"(Re)Learning Love"
by Jameelah Jones

LOVE AS LABYRINTH
PRESLEY THOMAS

A labyrinth is a maze that you can't get lost in. Movement through a labyrinth can be an act of prayer. The most famous one is laid into the floor of Chartres Cathedral in France. At its center is a flower with a winding path leading to it in four quadrants.

This is where love starts. Movement. And everyone's movement will look different. Even if it's only lifting a finger, even if our hearts feel too broken to love anymore or embrace what or who has harmed us. Acknowledge that, too.

These instructions aren't written down. They are found in our bodies, and spirits, and experiences of love, and faith or lack thereof. Where is your body now? Where is the Spirit? Can you feel it?

Not all labyrinths are meant to be walked. Some can be traced or meditated upon as a pattern. They are both complex and singular. The entrance is also the exit. You are meant to consider as you go the journey, meandering and circuitous. It is never the same for anyone. The labyrinth prayer journey depends on the experiences we hold in our bodies and where our minds go.

This, too, is Spirit. Our lives are rarely straight and ordered. Like the path of a labyrinth, it wanders. So too does love. We try to force it sometimes, but it doesn't work. Love is a labyrinth; it moves, and its reasoning may change, but the goal itself is not wanting or gaining, but love alone. When love finds love, we will see each other more, not less. Nor will we ask what parts of ourselves to hide.

Lord, help me to move. Even if it's only a little. Teach me what I need to know about how to love myself and others even though there has been pain. Amen.

This devotion was adapted from
"The Heart that Moves: Love as Labyrinth"
by Presley Thomas

AS YOURSELF

KEVIN GARCIA

Love is patient, love is kind, it isn't jealous, it doesn't brag, it isn't arrogant,
it isn't rude, it doesn't seek its own advantage, it isn't irritable, it doesn't keep a record
of complaints, it isn't happy with injustice, but it is happy with the truth.
Love puts up with all things, trusts in all things, hopes for all things,
endures all things. Love never fails. As for prophecies, they will be brought to an end.
As for tongues, they will stop. As for knowledge, it will be brought to an end.

1 Corinthians 13:4-8 (CEB)

1 Corinthians 13 is a classic text that always gets read at weddings. So much so that it has almost lost its meaning. But let's revisit this text as a prescription for how we should treat ourselves.

Do you know the reason we judge other people? Or the reason we are impatient or unkind to others? It is because we judge ourselves. It's because we are impatient and unkind to ourselves.

Have you ever said or thought "I should be... [anything]"? I should be more active. I should be more frugal. I should be kinder, better. I should be a better activist. I should, I should, I should...

Who said? Who said you had to be anything? This, again, is that capitalist love mindset where you have to perform a certain way in order to secure love. But that isn't how God works.

If God is love, then God is all the things we listed above. Patient. Kind. Not jealous. Not irritable.

'What would happen if we had that attitude toward ourselves? What if we were patient with ourselves when we screwed up? What if we were kind to ourselves when we didn't hit the mark we wanted to? What if we try to release jealousy? What if we don't even insist on our own ways when it comes to ourselves? What if life just happens, and we release our expectations of how we think it all should go?

This beloved passage from 1 Corinthians 13 contains step-by-step instructions on how we should act towards ourselves. And as we practice these ideals, knowing we aren't going to get them perfect, we can see how the virtues therein begin to work their way into how we treat the world around us.

How can you bear all things, hope all things, endure all things when it comes to your own person? How can you love yourself through your own impatience and imperfections? And how can you rejoice in the fact that all of it is beloved? Can you find ways to release radical self-compassion over your full self? Try it out. It may surprise you.

God, you are patient and kind.
You bear all things, hope all things, endure all things.
And because you do, I have already.
I have already overcome because you have overcome my imperfections and called
me good. You rejoice in the nicks and bruises and cracked parts of my person,
and You rejoice in it all.
Help me be radically present to the reality of your kindness in me. May your love in
me rise up and move me to speak against wrongdoing and celebrate truth when I see it.
May I love myself through my failures and release radical self-compassion. May I feel
your love rise in me in ways I have never felt before.
Amen.

This devotion was adapted from
"As Yourself"
by Kevin Garcia

CHAPTER 9
Purity & Sex

I was twelve when I first saw the skit performed at summer camp. A girl stood in the center of the room holding a flower. One by one, boys came up to rip off a petal until she was holding a naked stem, which she then offered to her dismayed "husband." Before I knew any better, that skit was an innocent way to portray sex and marriage. As a child, it made cartoon sense, but as a teen and then young adult, it just served to shame me for what my body needed and what my heart desired. It reduced my personhood down to the sex history I must one day provide.

Purity culture is damaging to *everyone*. Traditional Christian teachings about sex and sexuality are often the most difficult to unlearn because the whole experience of sexuality has just been replaced with shame. It's the shame, and it's the realization that sex is pervasively intertwined with all of human life—our social and romantic connections, dynamics of power and of play.

Sex touches every single thing there is to deconstruct. So once we begin pulling on that string, we soon discover that sexuality is the Great Unraveler. We're not just undoing the hold of purity culture—we are also unraveling white supremacy behind the patriarchy in the Church, the misogyny, the homophobia… the everything.

The following authors help unlock some of those tightly closed doors in our minds, pointing to a more authentic experience and expression of sexuality.

We invite you in.

RECLAIMING THE
PURITY OF SEX
JESSICA KANTROWITZ

At noon on the following day, as their journey brought them close to the city, Peter went up on the roof to pray. He became hungry and wanted to eat. While others were preparing the meal, he had a visionary experience. He saw heaven opened up and something like a large linen sheet being lowered to the earth by its four corners. Inside the sheet were all kinds of four-legged animals, reptiles, and wild birds.
A voice told him, "Get up, Peter! Kill and eat!"
Peter exclaimed, "Absolutely not, Lord! I have never eaten anything impure or unclean."
The voice spoke a second time, "Never consider unclean what God has made pure."
Acts 10:9-15 (CEB)

I think it's telling that when we think of Christianity and purity, we associate it with being a virgin till marriage, at which point sex suddenly becomes good and ordained.

I was helping out at a youth group meeting once, when the youth pastor read a story about a girl who owned a beautiful new pair of sneakers. My heart sank as I recognized the beginning of a familiar allegory. Boys kept coming and asking to wear the girl's sneakers, and she didn't really want them to, but she kept saying yes until they became all dirty and worn. Finally came the boy who the girl *really* wanted to share her sneakers with, but he was sad that they were so used up.

I felt like I was going to be sick. I knew some—if not many—of the kids in that group had already had sex. *I* had already had sex. And there was the youth pastor telling the girls in particular that we were used up, dirty things that our future spouses would be disappointed in—that *God* was disappointed in.

And what about those in the group who had been sexually abused? Those whose bodies had been touched against their will and who now had their deepest fears confirmed—that they were soiled and ruined, that they would never be truly loved.

Let me tell you this: Your sexual history does not make you impure. Your genitals are not a dirty sneaker. It is your heart before God that makes you pure or impure. And let me say this loudly because I did not have the courage to say it back then to that youth minister: *Do not call unclean that which God has made pure.*

God created us as sexual beings, and I do not believe that God despises us or sees us as dirty when we have consensual sex—even if it is outside the bounds that our church prescribes. And I believe that God wants us all, regardless of our beliefs on this subject, to be freed from shame.

God speaks this word over every aspect of ourselves, our sexuality included:
"Do not call anything impure that God has made clean."

This devotion was adapted from
"Reclaiming Our Purity"
by Jessica Kantrowitz

DECOLONIZING SEX

JO LUEHMANN

> *Then Peter spoke up, "Explain this riddle to us."*
> *Jesus said, "Don't you understand yet? Don't you know that everything that goes into*
> *the mouth enters the stomach and goes out into the sewer? But what goes out of the*
> *mouth comes from the heart. And that's what contaminates a person in God's sight.*
> *Out of the heart come evil thoughts, murders, adultery, sexual sins, thefts, false*
> *testimonies, and insults. These contaminate a person in God's sight. But eating without*
> *washing hands doesn't contaminate in God's sight."*

Matthew 15:15-20 (CEB)

In the above passage, Jesus is talking to some scribes and Pharisees about his disciples not washing their hands before eating. Religious leaders want to know why he doesn't tell them to keep with the traditions of the elders. Jesus responds by telling them they break God's commandments with their commitment to tradition. (A reminder here that Jesus also said all the commandments are summarized in two commands: "Love God, and love others as yourself.")

So breaking those commandments in order to uphold a commitment to tradition means holding onto traditions that keep us from loving God and/ or loving others.

Jesus then calls the religious leaders hypocrites for being so committed to tradition that they fail to love God and love others, and he reminds them that their worship is in vain (because using the Lord's name in vain is about using religion to harm others — not saying "God damn"). Then Jesus says it isn't what goes into a man's mouth that defiles a man, but what comes out of his heart. So it's not all about "doing the right things," but having loving motivations.

Peter asks Jesus to explain what he meant, and Jesus pretty much says, 'You still don't get it either?' And then he says something to the effect of 'whatever goes into your mouth goes into the belly and ends up in the toilet. But out of your heart come: Evil thoughts, murder, adultery, fornication, theft, false witness, blasphemies.'

Before we get into the word used here to speak of fornication, please look at that list and notice how every single one of those acts (except fornication as we understand it today) actively harms another human being. There is no denying that any one of those (again, except fornication) is not aligned with "love God, love others." In their original meanings in their original written language, each of the things Jesus lists actively and clearly harms another person. But to say that "fornication" as we understand it *today* actively harms others is a stretch.

So let's look at the original word that was translated to "fornication"—Πορνεία (porneia)—which literally means "illicit sexual intercourse." Fornication as we understand it today, however, means voluntary sexual intercourse between two consenting unmarried adults (per the dictionary). So, not quite the same thing, right?

So now we need to know—what is *illicit* sexual intercourse? Well, it depends who you ask. Per Levitical sexual ethics (Lev. 18), illicit sexual intercourse violations entailed: incest, intercourse during menstruation, adultery, child sacrifice, male-male anal rape, and bestiality. (A reminder that ancient people only deemed procreative sex in the confines of marriage as acceptable and required the woman to be a virgin, since this ensured that the baby would inherit their legitimate father's wealth and possessions.)

But does that mean that other sex not mentioned was "not ok" or that it didn't happen in biblical times? Well, no. It just means it wasn't relevant to the conversations they were having because it simply didn't affect them. They didn't care if two people having consensual sex couldn't procreate.

The obsession with policing women's sexuality and bodies had everything to do with protecting inheritance, and very little to do with sex and sexuality.

The obsession with ensuring men had sex had everything to do with passing down an inheritance, and very little to do with sex and sexuality.

These biblical conversations about sex were not about pleasure, our human experience, or even biology; they were practical conversations about who is getting what when dad dies or how-can-we-ensure-that-son-is-truly-his. Nowadays, we have a lot more information about biology, sexuality, gender, anthropology, sociology, and ethics. So we can gather our sexual ethics from a more reliable source than the Bible. Especially considering that the Bible technically allows for awful things like raping women (Deut. 21:10-14, Deut. 22:28-29, 2 Sam. 11), the stoning of a woman who's been raped (Deut. 22:23-29), sex slavery (Ex 21:7-8, Num. 31:18), and non-consensual polygamy (pretty much all of Genesis, 2 Sam. 5:13, 1 Kings 11:1-3).

Sex positivity advocates that all consensual, respectful sex—where nobody is being harmed—is holy (a reminder here that children cannot consent to sex). It promotes the understanding that exploring our sexuality is both healthy and absolutely natural.

Shame, fear, and guilt surrounding sex and sexuality haven't served anyone throughout history. In fact, those attitudes toward sex have caused greater trauma around sexuality, as well as an inability to advocate for (and even understand) what healthy, appropriate sexuality is. Sex positivity is the only way to approach sexuality where "love God, love others" is our actual, honest stance.

Have you been indoctrinated to believe that sex is bad unless it is between a married man and woman? How has that belief harmed your relationship with sex? How can we ensure sex is not used as a weapon against us or against others?

This devotion was adapted from
"Decolonizing Traditional Christianity"
by Jo Luehmann

DIVINE BODIES CREATED
IN GOD'S IMAGE
JULIA NUSBAUM

You are the one who created my innermost parts;
you knit me together while I was still in my mother's womb.
I give thanks to you that I was marvelously set apart.
Your works are wonderful—I know that very well.
Psalm 139:13-14 (CEB)

Where I grew up, in the rural Midwest, the non-denominational evangelical church had the "cool" youth group. It had the youth pastor who sported Chuck Taylor sneakers and zip-up hoodies. It had an entire building dedicated to its youth group. And in that building, there were basketball courts and even a coffee shop. If you were a Christian kid in my community, this was *the* spot.

But what I didn't understand was that they also had a culture of teaching young women and men to be ashamed of their bodies, their sexuality, and everything that came with those loaded topics. I attended that youth group Sunday after Sunday, hearing sermons that would stay with me for a very long time.

What I learned in that youth group followed me to college, making me afraid of relationships and so often ashamed of my own body. I hid from myself and from others. I hid parts of my personality, too, because I didn't know how to reconcile the God I was given in that Midwestern church with the God I was learning about as I studied religion—a God who didn't want me to be afraid of myself, my creativity, my sexuality. Rather, a God who had crafted and created me in an image of wonder and likeness.

The hard-edged God of my childhood has slowly slipped away in my adult years. Replaced with a God more mysterious, but also more loving.

And my body has become my own. Something I love and know and take care of. Something that is just as wonderful (and mysterious) as the God who crafted it.

Perhaps the greatest thing I have learned in this lifelong journey to claim my body as my own is that my body is a holy place. It always felt a little cliché to call my body God's temple, but it is holy nonetheless.

Our bodies and our sexuality and our spiritual beings are all connected. We cannot be one without the others. My body, your body, every body—is good and holy. If you are out there hating your body because of words you heard years ago in a church, or because of cultural expectations, or because your body has been used without your permission, remember that it is still good.

You are still good. You are an image of the Divine.

This devotion was adapted from
"Divine Bodies Created in God's Image"
by Julia Nusbaum

1888

108

108

EVEN FOR A SEX WORKER

REV. LURA GROEN

I have the freedom to do anything, but not everything is helpful. I have the freedom to do anything, but I won't be controlled by anything. Food is for the stomach and the stomach is for food, and yet God will do away with both. The body isn't for sexual immorality but for the Lord, and the Lord is for the body. God has raised the Lord and will raise us through his power. Don't you know that your bodies are parts of Christ? So then, should I take parts of Christ and make them a part of someone who is sleeping around? No way! Don't you know that anyone who is joined to someone who is sleeping around is one body with that person? The scripture says, The two will become one flesh. The one who is joined to the Lord is one spirit with him. Avoid sexual immorality! Every sin that a person can do is committed outside the body, except those who engage in sexual immorality commit sin against their own bodies. Or don't you know that your body is a temple of the Holy Spirit who is in you? Don't you know that you have the Holy Spirit from God, and you don't belong to yourselves? You have been bought and paid for, so honor God with your body.

1 Corinthians 6:12-20 (CEB)

What if Paul's words here are true even for a sex worker? Paul messes up gender and sex stuff all the time (I just have to accept it to preach on him). In this passage from his first letter to the church in Corinth, he's only talking to the men.

When I am preaching on Paul, and he acts a fool like he does here talking about fornication and sex work, I always like to go back and identify the central truths he is communicating, *then remind him of them.* Paul is not an authority on my body or my sexuality. He is, however, an authority on the grand themes of the relationship between God and humanity.

He just isn't so good at practically applying them to anyone other than men with status.

Your bodies are good and holy, temples of the Holy Spirit. All of them. Men's bodies, women's bodies, nonbinary bodies. Cis bodies and trans bodies. Disabled bodies. Trauma surviving bodies. All bodies. Holy and good, both the honored ones and the bodies sinned against by racism, sexism, transphobia, assault, poverty, and all the powers of evil in the world. They all carry the Holy Spirit; they all bear the image of God.

So, when I preach this text (and I never let it be read in church without at least referencing this in my sermons), I remind Paul that he knows all bodies are dwelling places of the Holy Spirit. I would then ask him to listen to Oprah's Golden Globes speech and consider the corporate ways we sin against Black bodies, against women's bodies, against gender non-conforming bodies, against bodies living in poverty. I would ask him to reconsider what he thinks a sin against the temple of God is and how a woman living in poverty and forced into sex work, or even choosing it willingly, deserves our care and deserves to be honored as bearing the image of God.

This devotion was adapted from
"Even for a Sex Worker"
by Rev. Lura Groen

PURITY CULTURE
& ASEXUALITY
REV. BAILEY BRAWNER

You are utterly beautiful, my dearest;
there's not a single flaw in you.
Song of Solomon 4:7 (CEB)

I used to be confused about asexuality because I was immersed in purity culture—religious institutions and people who were telling me that I needed to wait, save my body for my future husband. I remember that I just didn't find it that hard. I didn't feel the same 'sexual urges' they were telling me I'd be struggling with. I was completely fine waiting for whatever prince on a horse would come sweep me off my feet one day.

Years later, I learned the word for how I was feeling: asexual. I wasn't pious for not wanting to have sex, but because of the way that I was taught to "properly" use my body, I thought I was somehow set apart. Over time, I had to unlearn the things I was taught to feel shameful about, hide, or "save."

My brain had been trained to see sex in a certain way and to have certain expectations for how to do it (no pun intended). These teachings, which we often collectively refer to as purity culture, led me to an adulthood full of having to figure things out, when I could have been doing the work much earlier in life.

As an asexual person, I had to learn that asexuality is not the same as celibacy. Celibacy is a choice, a choice that queer and straight people alike can make. Asexuality is a sexual orientation, undetermined by one's sexual history. For folks in the queer community especially, societal and religious norms have given us no insight, much less affirmation, for how we can experience pleasure.

Whether you are in a relationship, having sex, choosing to be celibate, or wherever else you may find yourself in this season—you deserve to enjoy your body. You deserve to see God in the freedom God has given you to feel, to love, to live. You deserve to use your brain to make decisions about sex yourself, rather than be told to look at a very cherry-picked sentence or two in scripture to determine how you are to use your body.

Your worth is not defined by your sexual history.

Your worth is not defined by who you have sex with.

Your worth is not defined by how often you have sex.

Your worth is not defined by your libido.

You are of sacred worth.

God created your body for you. Just as God created the heavens and the earth, God created each of us, and God called it good. God called us good. God called our bodies good. And God continues to call us good, bodies and all. God has given us freedom to be free, to choose. Nobody—no church, no pastor, no institution—can take that choice away from you.

Your body is sacred.

Your body is beloved.

Your body is of sacred worth.

Your body is good.

Holy Creator,
You formed us in your image, and you called us good. You have given us freedom and
liberation, allowing us to experience pleasure in many forms. Help us, Creator, by
reminding us that we are of sacred worth.
Amen.

This devotion was adapted from
"Asexuali-Tea"
by Rev. Bailey Brawner

CHAPTER 10
LGBTQIA+

It is worth noting that this is our biggest chapter in the book. As editors of this project, we have interrogated our reasoning: Are we overcompensating for the lack of queer Christian voices in Christian literature? Or are we just so excited that we can't contain ourselves? Or are we maybe unable to whittle it down further because as two queer people ourselves, we can't bear to let any of these messages go unheard?

Yes.

In this chapter, our authors share a wide range of reflections—from the freedom of queering their theology to reflections on their journeys of beholding themselves as *good* and *beloved*.

It is important for everyone, not just queer folks, to read faith literature written from the perspective of queer writers or at the very least mentions queer people in a positive or even neutral light. So this section is *especially* for our queer siblings, but not just for them. Because queering theology or queering the traditional faith experience is liberating for everyone.

We invite you in.

CELEBRATE LOVE

ASHLEY DETAR BIRT

We have known and have believed the love that God has for us.
God is love, and those who remain in love remain in God and God remains in them.
This is how love has been perfected in us, so that we can have confidence on the Judgment
Day, because we are exactly the same as God is in this world. There is no fear in love,
but perfect love drives out fear, because fear expects punishment. The person who is
afraid has not been made perfect in love. We love because God first loved us.
Those who say, "I love God" and hate their brothers or sisters are liars.
After all, those who don't love their brothers or sisters whom they have seen can hardly
love God whom they have not seen! This commandment we have from him:
Those who claim to love God ought to love their brother and sister also.

1 John 4:16-21 (CEB)

"Love the sinner, hate the sin."

I've heard that phrase more often than I would have liked. People who I care for very much, who have acted as friends towards me, have said this to my face regarding my sexual orientation. As a person, they find me funny or charming or warm or smart. This one aspect of my life, however—my queerness—doesn't mesh with their expectations for what they've been taught about God, so they must reject it. It's okay to love me as long as they separate the good parts of me from the parts they have deemed unacceptable.

This isn't how God loves us, though. It isn't how any love should work. Love isn't about finding the parts of someone to love and throwing out the rest; it's about loving without fear, without hatred. We are all created by God, all loved by God, and all called to love God.

In order to do this, we must show each other love, for that is how God is revealed. Not only does this connect us to one another through God, but it also reminds us of the treatment and care we deserve. We all deserve the kind of love that allows us to see God. One cannot give that if they're busy figuring out how to "hate our sin."

What's more, to "hate the sin" in the case of sexual orientation is to hate love itself; a person's sexuality is part of their whole self. How can we love someone if we hate a part of them? As the text says, "Those who claim to love God ought to love their brother and sister also" (1 John 4:21, CEB). This sentiment can and should be applied to all people: parents, siblings, friends, and significant others alike—all the significant and the seen parts of life. May all affection and affirmation shown between them be valued just as the one unseen is valued.

Remember that the love in your life, regardless of what it may look like, is not sinful, but inspired by God. Celebrate the blessing of your capacity to love.

This devotion was adapted from
"Celebrate! An LGBTQ+ Devotional"
by Ashley DeTar Birt

BEHOLD YOURSELF

EMANUEL H. BROWN

In African Spiritual traditions of the Yoruba people, the Orisha are worshipped as a pantheon of gendered, non-gendered, and multi-gendered deities through song, dance, story, and ritual. As I understand it, being in a relationship with these avatars is designed to help us hone our spiritual gifts and be in right relationship with each other and nature.

Oshun—most attributed to the rivers, beauty, fertility, and pleasure—has become a divine guide on how to deepen, transform, and release relationships. Often depicted as a beautiful woman draped in gold, Oshun carries several instruments representing her work in the world, including a mirror. While her mirror can be associated with the dangers of vanity, a deeper look may find us asking the question: What does it mean to behold our reflection?

As a Black Caribbean trans nonbinary person, beholding my reflection has not been an easy task. For so long the person staring back at me was not ME. It was the version of me crafted by my family, friends, and society at large. It was a me deeply disconnected from my body, emotions, and spiritual purpose. It was a me able to code switch and morph into others' expectations. It was a me existing to survive.

Then I discovered—my *community* was my reflection.

These were the people who held me through grief, celebrated my accomplishments, offered me accountability, and kept me close to hope. When I couldn't see myself, I could look at the lives of my teachers to understand my own arc of transformation. Where I lacked the ability to feel my wholeness, I found courage from the gender transgressors who became more of themselves by changing their names, their clothes, and at times their bodies. Where I could not find myself desirable, I was able to lean in to the touch of lovers affirming my right to exist.

I began to believe the version of me I saw reflected in my community. I allowed myself to take in the narrative they weaved for me. I reclaimed my reflection. Hazy at first, I was able to fill out the definition over time: my father's nose, my mother's eyes, the dimples I share with a brother, my complexion just a little lighter than his but darker than my older sisters.' I was able to survey all I was and all the things shaping me. I no longer disguised my mistakes, and I found my ability to make amends hidden in my heart.

A daily practice, I notice the subtle changes in my skin, brightness of my eyes, how tall I stand, and my ability to inhabit my roundness. I take in the perfection of it, breathing out the judgment. On my worst days, my vision becomes blurred, and I call up the words of my beloveds to help me remember. On my best days I can look out my window at a beautiful thing and say "YES, I am that."

Sit, stand, or lay in front of a mirror.
Take in all that you can see or imagine there. Name what you notice out loud.
Breathe in your perfection and breathe out judgement ten times.

This devotion was adapted from
"Radical Relationships"
by Emanuel H. Brown

FAILED BY FAMILY
REV. JES KAST

More than anything you guard, protect your mind, for life flows from it.
Ecclesiastes 4:23 (CEB)

Choosing to come out to family as queer is always a brave decision. Each family is so different. Even if you come from one of the most supportive and loving families, it still is brave to choose to tell the truth of who you are to your family. Some people have beautiful stories of family that increased their support after they came out, but for many of us in the LGBTQIA+ community, many of us also know what it's like to be disowned by family members who fail us.

There is a particular pain when family turns their back on us. It is a confusing pain because it begs the question: How can I choose to be in relationship with a family member who has failed me?

This is an important question that each person answers differently. The book of Ecclesiastes is full of wisdom, and it offers us one way to answer it: guard your heart, for the vitality of our lives comes from the soft and strong essence of our core.

Being in relationship with people takes vulnerability and risk—no matter who you are. If the one we are being vulnerable with is unable to handle the truth of our lives and instead continues to turn their back on our hearts in harsh ways, it would be wise for us to reevaluate how close we want to be to that person. Some of us may even make the painful, but often freeing choice to cut off relationships with family members who have hurt us. Some of us will choose to build a new relationship. There isn't one right way to do this. It's muddy, and we'll get a little dirty, but dirty should never diminish our dignity.

The good news is that Jesus models for us a new way of being family with each other. He picked people to be his brothers, sisters, and siblings and talked about a new community. The Jesus community wasn't always related by blood, but by love. Jesus said that people would recognize his followers by how they love each other. Love, not blood, is the mark of family. Love is the measure we are given in how we want people to relate to us.

These are hard decisions that are reevaluated over time, but if we keep love at the forefront, we will be able to protect our wild and precious hearts and find community. Community will literally save and support us. And you are worthy of that type of love!

God, guide me so that I may receive and give love.
Give me a community that supports me through thick and thin. Amen.

This devotion was adapted from
"The Power of Praise"
by Rev. Jes Kast

QUEER LOVE IS HOLY
JONAH VENEGAS

As a queer person of faith, I wanted to write a reflection I longed to hear when I was younger, so if you need to hear this, this is for you.

The first time I really felt truly seen as a queer Asian person was when I watched the anime *Yuri!!! On Ice*. Then, the anime *Banana Fish* catalyzed the opening of a space where the veil between here and heaven grew thin for me. In *Banana Fish*, Eiji Okumura arrives in New York City as a 19-year old photojournalist assistant reporting on street gangs when he meets Ash, an 18-year old gang leader who has been groomed, abused, and manipulated by the Corsican mob. Together, with a number of allies they make along the way, these two uncover a large drug conspiracy.

Perhaps what is most striking about their story is the way Ash and Eiji's relationship grows and evolves along its trajectory. On the surface, they are nothing alike, and yet they gravitate towards each other. But as time passes, the two become inseparable, a true example of soulmates. It was breathtaking for me to see how they loved each other so fiercely and steadfastly—selflessly.

The depth of these characters' love went beyond anything I'd ever witnessed, both in fiction and reality, and it pierced my own soul. At one point in the story, Ash even wonders aloud how Eiji can love someone so broken, to which Eiji responds: "Even if the world turns on you, I'll always be by your side." And it's not a naïve or delusional promise either.

Their love for each other is something I haven't been able to get out of my head. Everything about their relationship and their love lives up to every sermon, every article, every message I've ever heard on what a good, loving relationship is supposed to look like. Ash and Eiji sacrifice and give of themselves for each other, and they make each other better by shoring up the strengths and weaknesses of the other.

Their relationship is everything I was taught to seek after in church. So to me, their love is holy. The way they love and relate to each other even reminds me of the way Jesus related to the world during his time on earth. He was both fierce and tender, kind and savvy. He both cared deeply for those considered unlovable and ardently protected the vulnerable.

If I'm being honest, I would be hard-pressed to come up with a love that reminds me of Jesus more than this queer anime couple's relationship. To me, their queer love is holy by its very nature; I believe it reflects Jesus exactly the way I was always taught in church.

I think many of us have conditioned ourselves or been conditioned to only be open to experiences with the Divine in pre-approved times and places arbitrarily deemed holy enough or spiritual enough—but I don't think that's actually how God moves. Jesus tells us in the book of John that the Spirit blows where it pleases like the wind, so who are we as humans to say when or where we can or cannot experience God?

If it weren't for being open to meeting the Divine in unconventional places, I never would have learned any of the things She taught me, and I certainly never would have experienced the holiness of Ash and Eiji's love. Because everything They created is holy. Art is holy. Anime is holy. Queer love is holy. Each and every story we see or read or experience is holy, because they all emerge from people—people made in the image of the Divine.

So, let's keep seeing the presence of God, and let's keep ourselves open to meeting Them in places you wouldn't expect, but in the places He knows you most need to find Him. Because God can create thin meeting places anywhere, and that means anything can be holy.

God, thank you for finding us in the places You know we need to meet You. Help us to expand our perceptions of You, to hear You, see You, and feel You. Help us to remember that everything You have made is holy.

This devotion was adapted from
"Everything Is Holy"
by Jonah Venegas

Runaway Bunny Love
AUSTEN HARTKE

Where could I go to get away from your spirit?
Where could I go to escape your presence?
If I went up to heaven, you would be there.
If I went down to the grave, you would be there too!
If I could fly on the wings of dawn,
stopping to rest only on the far side of the ocean—
even there your hand would guide me;
even there your strong hand would hold me tight!
If I said, "The darkness will definitely hide me;
the light will become night around me,"
even then the darkness isn't too dark for you!
Nighttime would shine bright as day,
because darkness is the same as light to you!

Psalm 139:7-12 (CEB)

When you were little, did you ever read the story of the runaway bunny? It's all about this baby rabbit who decides to run away from home. When he tells his mother, she says "If you run away, I will run after you." The baby bunny says, "If you run after me, I will become a flower," and the mother bunny says, "Then I will become a gardener." The baby bunny says he will become a bird, and the mother bunny says then she will become a tree that the bird can always come home to. No matter what the baby bunny does, or where he goes, his mother finds a way to be there—sometimes in the background, and sometimes right up close.

When I read this part of Psalm 139, all I can think about is how God is just like that mother bunny. If we ascend to heaven, God is there. If we go down into whatever the opposite of heaven is (there's just a bit of debate about that!), then God is there too. If we fly as far away from God as we think we can get—guess what? God's still there, and God's waiting for us.

I know a lot of LGBTQIA+ Christians who worry about whether God can still love them if they're gay, or bisexual, or transgender, or asexual—and I always love to point them to these verses. God can do whatever God wants, and what God wants to do is love you! Of course, sometimes we feel like God is a long, long way away. We feel this urge to get closer to God, and that urge is good. But I think it's important to recognize that God hasn't gone anywhere, and really—neither have we. When God feels far away, that's a good time to realize that we've been acting like the baby bunny, pretending to be what we're not, and trying to get away from a love that's always nearby.

So open up your eyes, remember that God loves you for who you are and not for what you could be, and see if you can find the ways the Spirit is following you!

This devotion was adapted from
"Psalms & Self-Care"
by Austen Hartke

THE DEPTH & COMPLEXITY
OF IDENTITY
REV. BAILEY BRAWNER

Set me as a seal over your heart,
as a seal upon your arm,
for love is as strong as death,
passionate love unrelenting as the grave.
Its darts are darts of fire—
divine flame!
Rushing waters can't quench love;
rivers can't wash it away.
Song of Solomon 8:6-7 (CEB)

Part of my work as a pastor involves starting conversations with my congregations to help move them forward into attitudes of acceptance and understanding. It's beautiful, and it's also challenging sometimes. We had a workshop discussing our church and human sexuality, and I invited people to share their names and their pronouns. People obliged, but I got some pushback after: *Why is it necessary? We all know each other. We'd ask if we had a question about someone.*

The key difference between my intention in the exercise and those who received it revolved around the issue of assumptions. We give our pronouns because it gives people an opportunity to tell others how they identify, how they want to be named. The traditionally feminine presenting person has an opportunity to say, 'Hey I use they/them pronouns,' etc. Or maybe the person in your class you've known all year has the freedom to try on an identity they haven't been able to vocalize yet. It gives each of us an opportunity to clarify to others how we want to be called.

No matter what we know about someone, we can't stop there. When we stop asking questions and working to know someone better, we put people in boxes; this allows us to keep them in our mind exactly as they are, for as long as we want to keep them there. It stifles growth, and it pushes away creativity and newness. And when we are there, boxing people, we can't celebrate them. We can't put people in boxes, and we can't put God in boxes either.

There's so much beauty in the complexity. There's so much beauty in our difference, our queerness, our uniqueness. Honoring God means honoring that God is too big for labels, for an acronym, for whatever something or someone looks like on the outside. We should be celebrating that reality.

We who are created in the image of God, the *Imago Dei*, are created with the same level of intentional complexity. We are being given the gift to honor God's fullness by living out ours. And that is a gift for everyone.

May we remember that our fullness, our difference, and our layers make us human; and they make us children of God, the one whose grace abounds, whose works astound, and who is always worthy of praise.

You are sacred and loved.
Your body is good.
Your diversity is beauty.
Your voice is Spirit at work.
Your intimacy is powerful.
Your sexuality is yours.
You deserve to be seen.
You are seen.
You are better than 'normal.'
You are a beloved child of God.

This devotion was adapted from
"Asexuali-Tea"
by Rev. Bailey Brawner

PSALM 139

EMILY JOY ALLISON

You are the one who created my innermost parts;
you knit me together while I was still in my mother's womb.
I give thanks to you that I was marvelously set apart.
Your works are wonderful—I know that very well.

Psalm 139:13-14 (CEB)

I think it's important to reflect on Psalms like these, especially to celebrate a time like Pride Month. Pride itself, while a celebration, started as a protest. It started as a vehicle of public grief and lament at the ways that queer people were treated by society and the state, as a chorus of voices crying out in the wilderness that things were not as they should or could be.

And sadly, that is sometimes even truer in our churches than it is in the world at large. Often, our churches are the most dangerous, oppressive, and life-draining places for LGBTQIA+ folks; and that is by design, rather than by accident.

But the Psalms tell a different story about the goodness of our created selves than either our homophobic culture or our homophobic faith communities do. Psalm 139 reminds us that we are made as we should have been, in all the glorious, resplendent, variations of human beings.

No one person is more fearfully made than another, especially not on the basis of what other sort of people they are attracted to. Later in this Psalm, the writer refers to themselves as "knit together" or, in another translation (NRSV), "intricately woven"—as in *on purpose*.

Not an accident. Not an afterthought. Exactly who you are, baked into the fabric of your being.

Let's celebrate who we are, protest injustice in our midst, and affirm to each other and to ourselves that we are fearfully, wonderfully, purposefully, gloriously made.

This devotion was adapted from
"Divine Space for Divine Emotions"
by Emily Joy Allison

MY GOD & YOUR GOD

HL HOLDER-BROWN

While the disciples were in hiding after the Crucifixion, Mary Magdalene and company were busy taking care of Jesus's body—taking care of Jesus even when they thought all their hopes and dreams had died with him. Even though they were grief stricken and heart broken. They showed more faith in those moments than the other disciples did—perhaps not for a lack of fear, but because they were able to channel their fear into doing something good.

Coming out can be absolutely terrifying—especially without the support of your faith community and/or family. Starting a relationship with someone you cannot even tell your parents about for fear of rejection and demonization is more than enough to make many queer folks not even try. But as someone who hasn't been out of the closet that long, let me tell you this: You can have hope that Jesus is for you. And though your faith community may intimidate you and tell you that you don't belong in the body of Christ—*you do belong.*

Mary Magdalene was looking for Jesus and taking care of him even when the rest of the disciples had given up hope. Then the resurrected Lord appeared to women first. Women, who were often marginalized in a patriarchal society and who didn't have much autonomy over their own lives. Jesus saw them, and they were important players in his inner circle. No one has exclusive ownership of Jesus. No one has exclusive ownership of God, regardless of their gender identity or sexuality. Mary Magdalene understood this more than most.

Through all of my doubts and wanderings, I keep coming back to think about the Resurrection and whether there's hope in something we cannot prove or understand. I still believe in resurrection and a Kingdom coming, and I hope in the here and now simply because I believe, I *know*, there must be more than this. And I know that I still believe in Jesus and in the Resurrection—that in the midst of death and suffering, new life will come. But it's hard sometimes.

God, who is my God and your God, is with you when you come out. This God who came to be with us in our humanity is with you when you start relationships that could result in losing your family and church community. This God who is my God and your God is with you when the relationships end. Because He is the God of Resurrection and Life. The God of new beginnings and new life.

This devotion was adapted from
"Children of God"
by HL Holder-Brown

LOVING FROM THE MARGINS

GENNIFER DORGAN

This is my commandment: love each other just as I have loved you.
No one has greater love than to give up one's life for one's friends.
John 15:12-13 (CEB)

But as it is, there are many parts but one body. So the eye can't say to the hand,
"I don't need you," or in turn, the head can't say to the feet, "I don't need you."
1 Corinthians 12:20-21 (CEB)

Jesus calls his disciples to be fellows in faith who love each other so much that one would willingly die to save another. As Paul emphasizes in 1 Corinthians, self-abnegating love that still affirms the value of every individual member of the Church is essential for fellowship with Jesus.

Reading these verses, I have often asked myself, "Is my love enough?" I am fortunate to be surrounded by loving family and friends, but very few of them share my faith. Christian practice is an overwhelmingly solitary experience for me. Sometimes I wish I had someone to read the Bible and pray with.

As a gay Christian, however, I am used to congregations telling me that they have no need of me. I believed for a long time that I would never experience the mutual apostolic love described by Jesus and Paul and would always be alienated from Christian fellowship in this life. Eventually, God blessed me by proving me wrong. A friend invited me to a Bible study group when I was in graduate school, where I made two dear friends who embrace me for who I am. At last, I had that coveted experience of being transported out of myself through fellowship in faith. Graduation separated us, but we continue to be near to each other in prayer.

Where I was growing up, people who went to church had been going together for generations. Now, faith communities are constantly being fragmented and re-forming.

It's hard being separated from my friends, but I know that we remain members of one body. And the modern world is not unlike the time of the first apostles: as we go forth, opening ourselves up to strangers, it poses both the danger of hostility *and* the promise of love.

This devotion was adapted from
"Loving from the Margins"
by Gennifer Dorgan

A Divine Affirmation
Scot Robinson

But Moses said to God, "If I now come to the Israelites and say to them,
'The God of your ancestors has sent me to you,' they are going to ask me,
'What's this God's name?' What am I supposed to say to them?"
God said to Moses, "I Am Who I Am. So say to the Israelites, 'I Am has sent me
to you.'" God continued, "Say to the Israelites, 'The Lord, the God of your ancestors,
Abraham's God, Isaac's God, and Jacob's God, has sent me to you.'
This is my name forever; this is how all generations will remember me.
Exodus 3:13-15 (CEB)

What a strong affirmation of self that God gives to Moses here: "I am who I am." At a moment when Moses needed the right words and actions to deliver God's message to the Israelites, God lets Moses know that he doesn't need to spice things up or morph God into something more palatable for the people.

This God's deliverance is motivated by divine faithfulness to the promises made to Abraham and the one who hears the cry of the oppressed—not the wants of royalty. In the truest sense, what could be more queer or non-conforming than that? What would it take for us to be able to fully affirm this statement and begin to love ourselves? This includes our bodies, our sexual orientation, our gender identity, and all those pieces of our identity that don't conform to what society has deemed fit.

All of these parts of our identity are also parts of the divinity we were created in; therefore, one can stand and affirm it, knowing that God honors the loving and affirmation of oneself. Shedding the shame and baggage that society has dumped on you is a difficult journey, so just saying "I am" is easier said than done.

Shame and guilt are the antithesis of the *imago dei*. Sonya Renee Taylor, who writes about "radical self-love" in relation to our bodies, addresses how our society can teach us that we always need to apologize for our selves and our bodies. However, Taylor's hope is that after all of this baggage is obliterated and we tear down the pillars of hierarchy within ourselves, we can then trust in the fact that what is left standing is our own divine enoughness, disconnected from any need for comparison (*Building a Radical Self-Love in an Age of Loathing*, 2018).

That divine enoughness is inherent in all of us no matter the size, sexual orientation, or gender identity. A lot of times, our churches and faith communities get things wrong when it comes to sexuality and gender. Theologian Pamela Lightsey writes that, as a gay black woman, she notices that the conversations in the Church around sexuality are often not guided by faith, but by the will of control (*The Biblical Crisis*, 2015).

This stems from the fear of the unknown; when this unknown is encountered, scripture is used not to "find out," but to "tell why." Lightsey recognizes an unwillingness to say "I don't know" in relation to human sexuality, when we truly don't always have the answers. Lightsey clues us in, however, on what we can do with what we do know: we can begin by loving ourselves as God has created us. In other words, stand boldly and say "I am who I am."

> How great is your love, Lord God, how wide is your mercy!
> Never let us board up the narrow gate that leads to life with rules or doctrines
> that you dismiss, but give us a Spirit to welcome all people with affection,
> so that your Church may never exclude secret friends of yours,
> who are included to the love of Jesus Christ, who came to save us all.
> Amen.

This devotion was adapted from
"(S)Exodus: Affirming Your Identity, Body, and Fight for Justice through Exodus"
by Scot Robinson

CHAPTER 11
Reframing God

One of the great joys and celebrations of reconstructing our imagery of God is that we can encounter God so much more often than before. We recognize God in places and faces we never could have dreamed of. With names and pronouns we never associated with God. In religions and other spiritual practices we did not expect to find God in.

When we are reconstructing our imagery of God, it can reveal in others a divinity that at first we could not recognize. If you have a learning experience that's anything like ours, reframing God's image will allow you to see Her in places and faces you never thought She could be.

This chapter is a celebration of finding new and more abundant images of God.

We invite you in.

FINDING THE FACE OF GOD
CINDY WANG BRANDT

*The unmistakable face of God shows up in the presence of the most
vulnerable and helpless among us.*

Over a meal, my daughter wondered what God looks like. She figured that
we will find out when we get to heaven.

If all we speak of the good news as just salvation to heaven, children—
who are far from pondering death—cannot grasp the hope that is within
their reach in the present.

Pete Rollins says that the Christian question is not whether there is
life after death, but whether there is life before death. Similarly, my daughter thinks she won't see the face of God until heaven. But nothing can be
further from the truth. I am reminded of something I posted on Facebook
after meeting my friend's newborn son, shortly after he was confirmed with
a Down Syndrome diagnosis:

As image bearers we can find glimpses of the Divine in our fellow
humankind. In the arts we explore the depths of his mystery. In academia,
we uncover the theological complexity and nuance. But always, the unmistakable face of God shows up in the presence of the most vulnerable and
helpless among us.

Holding my friend's baby was a taste of the Christian hope. In addition
to the heavenly scent that emanated from him (a mixture of sweet baby milk
breath and Johnson & Johnson soap), his slanted almond eyes and the extra
space separating his big toe from the others bore witness to his frail vulnerability.

I think we are often drawn to the innocence of babies precisely because
of their helplessness. They require tender care for their every need, and we

are most deeply satisfied when we give of ourselves. The circle of life is one of receiving and giving of love; back and forth, to and from. A baby coo or a lopsided sleepy grin is capable of melting the hardest of hearts. And a child's special needs only serve to amplify the exchange of love, drawing those around to give more of themselves. It is the essence of the gospel.

The truth is—those who are visibly poor, physically ill, or even babies with Down Syndrome bring the face of God to the forefront of our attention. They blatantly demand we encounter what Glennon Doyle once coined "the brutiful life." The harsh realities facing the future of my friend's baby somehow doesn't diminish the solid hope he promises through his riveting, soulful eyes. It is both brutal and beautiful.

Some of us are more reserved with our brutiful lives, and it takes extra work to excavate the face of God. We hold our secret pains within us until they threaten to tear us apart from the inside out. We pretend everything is okay for so long and so often that we have almost believed it ourselves. We don't ask, and we don't tell. We live in the shadows of our own lives, watching it play out as a disconnected reality, avoiding confrontation with the ghosts of our brokenness. We hide from the face of God.

I am convinced the Christian hope lies in life before death, given to us through pockets of love like the moment I held my friend's baby, who brings to surface the needs of humanity – to cry, laugh, sleep; to be fed, held, cared for, and loved. The world may regard the extra chromosome as a deficit, a falling short of humanity. But the gospel resides within him; the face of God is unmistakable, to show us all how to live more fully. In Matthew 25, Jesus says when we feed the hungry, it is as if we are feeding Jesus himself, the incarnation of God.

God is present in the margins.

This devotion was adapted from
"Finding the Face of God"
by Cindy Wang Brandt

WHERE LOVE IS, GOD IS
DANNY PRADA

But the fruit of the Spirit is love, joy, peace, patience, kindness, goodness, faithfulness, gentleness, and self-control. There is no law against things like this.
Galatians 5:22-23 (CEB)

If the Spirit is always responsible for producing Christ-like transformation in others, what does it say that this sort of transformation seems to be occurring—to a more or less equal extent—across all religious traditions? If God is always the source of good, then anywhere we see the fruits of the Spirit, we must acknowledge the power of the Spirit at work.

Experientially speaking, it's obvious that the transformative power of God has been active within a variety of different religious traditions, despite the varying dogmas they have. Salvation, therefore, is not a matter of affirming dogmas, but of living a life of union with God.

Before being labeled Christians, the earliest disciples of Jesus were known as "followers of the Way." Sadly, what began as a dynamic way of life eventually fossilized into a static system of beliefs. This is perhaps our greatest failure as a religion! Our own scriptures teach us that "final judgment" will not be predicated on the content of one's beliefs, but on the quality of one's love.

Thankfully, there is no such thing as "Christian" love or "Muslim" love or "Jewish" love. Love is love, and since love is taught in every religion, love belongs to no religion. God is love, and since love is found in other religions— God can be found there, too.

Christians believe that being formed in the way of love is an impossibility apart from the grace of God at work through the Spirit. It is this theological premise that allows the Christian to perceive God's salvific work far beyond the confines of their own tradition. This is why we affirm, with the

Apostle John, that everyone who loves has been born of God and knows God (1 John 4:7).

A few years ago, a friend of mine (who had converted to Christianity) reached out to me after the passing of his Muslim father. He was struggling with the thought of his father being in hell because he had not "accepted Jesus" during his lifetime. With tears in his eyes he looked at me and said, "All I know is that my dad lived more like Jesus than any of the Christians I know."

What does it mean that those who do not bear the name of Christ oftentimes seem to resemble him more than those who do? All we can say is that the wind of the Spirit is free to blow wherever it wishes.

Wherever I find love, I find God.

This devotion was adapted from
"Above Every Name"
by Danny Prada

LOVE IS NOT GENDERED
JAMEELAH JONES

God said to Moses, "I Am Who I Am.
So say to the Israelites, 'I Am has sent me to you.'"
Exodus 3:14 (CEB)

"God does not call us to conform to narrow gender stereotypes,
but to be conformed to the image of Christ."
Rachel Held Evans

In 2016, I spent the entire year working to break the habit of using "He" pronouns for God. I started prayers with "Mother/Father/Parent God." As I read scripture, I was checking myself for the male images I had in mind. I even replaced "he" with "God" when I was singing gospel songs. This was a small change that turned out to be one of the best spiritual decisions of my life. I figured this little experiment would lead to a small shift in my faith, or at the very least, a more inclusive use of language. But I wasn't expecting the drastic transformation of how I approach love.

Think about it. We often hear and speak of God's love being perfect, all-knowing, and necessary to our survival. We also have been socialized to see God as a man. And if we go further, we could also accept what *kind* of man we've been taught to picture God to be. So what does it mean when we attach a cisgender, heterosexual, white, male image to the vision of God's perfect love?

For me, it meant I expected God to take on the characteristics of men when it came to how I experienced Their love. I saw God as a strict father figure; so, like many kids, I spent a lot of time rebelling against my Father-in-the-sky who had so many rules for me. I took silences during prayer as

God's punishment or unwillingness to hear me. I had a very limited view of my body and the ways it could feel and express intimacy. Worst of all, my vision of love was limited to what men could provide.

To assume God is male or only imagine a male image of God is to limit the ways you can encounter and define love. The first step in radically changing the way we love is to question our literal image of God's perfect love. If there is no room to question where the male image of God comes from, there is no room to accept that we could be called to love deeper, much more differently, than what man can imagine.

God, forgive me for accepting a limiting version of you.
Help me break the habit of assuming you are a gendered being.
Open my heart to new ways to see you and new ways to experience your limitless love.

This devotion was adapted from
"(Re)Learning Love"
by Jameelah Jones

A GOD-THING
SUSAN COTTRELL

"It's a God-thing!"

I have said this many times along my faith journey. When I recognize something extraordinary, outside the norm, something especially coincidental or helpful or unexpected — *It must be a God-thing.* One day, I said it to a friend, and she sighed.

"Breathe in," she told me. "Breathe out. THAT'S a God-thing."

Ah, of course! God-things occur all around us, all the time—not just the occasional blips that my human brain sometimes recognizes, then identifies and labels a God-thing. At that point, I had no qualms about declaring this or that as God-things. I had not thought through the implications of declaring where God is or isn't, what is God's doing and what is not.

Now, all of that feels silly. I've seen and known a God who is much bigger (and kinder, and more loving) than my then smaller understanding allowed. Now, I'm in a whole new place. Now that my understanding of God has expanded (and my box for God has been shredded), I see God in ways I didn't before. I now see God in places—and in faces—that I didn't before. Isn't that a beautiful thing?

Now, I am able to recognize God's presence anywhere and anytime. I've decided to label it ALL a God-thing. Because it is.

This devotion was adapted from
"Searching for God in Religion"
by Susan Cottrell

FREEDOM IN WORSHIP

MEGAN JESSOP

But the time is coming—and is here!—when true worshippers will worship in spirit and truth. The Father looks for those who worship him this way. God is spirit, and it is necessary to worship God in spirit and truth.

John 4:23-24 (CEB)

In order to talk about God, we must understand that all our words fall short of understanding or conveying who, or what, God is.

To say that God is Father is not sufficient, because God is also Mother, amongst others. God consists of all things and is in all things. When placed into the context of the Trinity, there are the three forms—Father, Son, and Holy Spirit—that must also be considered in understanding God. One part cannot exist solely by itself.

We understand that our connections with God exist in a spiritual context. But what does it mean to worship God in spirit? What does it mean to worship God in truth? In the passage from John 4, Jesus is speaking to the woman at the well, the Samaritan woman who admits to him that she has had multiple affairs. Rather than passing judgment, Jesus speaks with her. An outsider woman, a sinner. This in itself is revolutionary.

In a closer look at that passage, delving into the Greek translations, we would find that that the Greek word for truth is *alétheia*. This word has often been used interchangeably with "reality." The word for Spirit is *pnuema* or "breath." The Greek word for worship is *proskuneo* which means "to lie prostrate." It's easy to look at these words and fit them into a religious paradigm—one like this woman at the well probably knew all too well.

But if we look even closer, we will see that to lie prostrate is more of a metaphor… it's more about the positioning of our lives than it is the ritual of being on our faces. It's about becoming less and allowing God to become more. It's about laying down our selfishness and allowing every single breath that we breath to become the reality of love. Because our breath is spirit, and God is Spirit. So with every breath, we breathe in the very nature and essence of God, which is love. And that love becomes our reality.

This devotion was adapted from
"A Week of Freedom"
by Megan Jessop

MEETING CHRIST IN YOUR
BREATH WITH HINDUISM
REV. DREW TUCKER

...the Lord God formed the human from the topsoil of the fertile land and blew
life's breath into his nostrils. The human came to life.
Genesis 2:7 (CEB)

What if I told you that my friends of other religious identities strengthened, rather than diluted, my faith in Jesus?

As a white, cisgender, straight, temporarily abled, middle-class male who happens to serve as University Pastor at Capital University (a historically Lutheran institution), I carry a lot of privilege. Part of my role is to care for the spiritual wellness of all students, faculty, and staff—not just the Lutherans and other Christians, but all people of all faiths. This doesn't mean I'm always the right person to meet those needs; in fact, it often means I need to connect students with other spiritual leaders (like rabbis, imams, gurus, priests, or counselors), as well as provide access to resources so they can fully practice their faith traditions. Frequently, when I share this with other Christians, they wonder, "But, isn't that a challenge to your own faith?"

Of course, some use "challenge" to mean a difficulty to reconcile what I've come to believe, while others are much more concerned that this "challenge" is an assault on the authority of Jesus in my life. But the answer to both is: Most often? No. This actually strengthens my Christian faith by showing me God's presence in places I've never explored.

For instance, in my work, I've come to know a number of Hindu folks who've shared with me Patanjali's Eight Limbs of Yoga. The yoga movements most common in the U.S.A. are actually only one limb of Patanjali's teaching, called *asana* (posture). Another essential component of yoga, per Patanjali, is *pranayama* (breath control), which seeks to control and connect with the *prana*, or life force.

The first time I heard this, it perked up my Sunday school ears. I'd heard about breath of life before, way back in Genesis. I remembered that God breathed into the earth creature, making it come alive. Then I remembered that, as a religion major in undergrad, I learned that the Hebrew word for breath is the same word for spirit. So, in other words, God breathed God's spirit into our lungs at creation, and our life force began with that ultimate reality as breath in our lungs.

For me, they point to the beauty of our breath in the Christian tradition. Of course, we must also remember that these are different traditions closely tied to cultural identity. Hindu practitioners may practice yoga, including pranayama, along with religious worship. We should learn from the traditions and practices of others, but Christians should be careful not to co-opt the practices and relabel them as Christianity.

What we as Christians can learn from Patanjali is that the life force, given to us with our very first breath, deserves attention. It deserves focus. It deserves a practice. That God breathed life into our lungs means that focusing on our breath is to center ourselves on a divine gift—the presence of the Holy Spirit, present with each inhale and exhale.

You can begin to acknowledge this divine accompaniment in your lungs and practice mindfulness with your breath. Simply spend time bringing attention to your breath, noticing what it feels like to breathe in and breathe out.

Each breath is a reflection of that first breath,
a taste of God's Spirit filling our lungs and igniting our life.

This devotion was adapted from
"Meeting Christ in Interfaith Relationships"
by Drew Tucker

CHAPTER 12
Community

I sometimes enjoy replacing "you" with "y'all" any time Jesus says it in the Gospels. When I make this small change, it becomes a community-driven gospel. I was talking to a friend about this, and she said that the English language is just so incredibly limiting. Many other languages have several different words to address others in second person, but we kind of... don't. Small, nuanced differences like that can carry huge, culture-defining meaning. Which leads me to believe that our limited capabilities for expressing community in words also limits our abilities to form community.

Jesus gave a personal command to love your neighbor as yourself, that is to say, love others well. To love our neighbor, we must have a depth of empathy for the unknown—both in others and in ourselves. To offer everyone dignity, kindness, and care is a radical kind of love we have yet to get right, especially if we've yet to learn how to extend that same love to ourselves. For how can we love others well if we have not truly loved ourselves?

We invite you in.

HEALING PARTS OF THE BODY
DEBORAH JIAN LEE

The parts of our body that are presentable don't need this. But God has put the body together, giving greater honor to the part with less honor so that there won't be division in the body and so the parts might have mutual concern for each other. If one part suffers, all the parts suffer with it; if one part gets the glory, all the parts celebrate with it.
1 Corinthians 12:24-26 (CEB)

In college, I toggled between two very different worlds. I devoted half of my time to my campus ministry, a predominantly white group that was culturally very different from my youth group. I loved this community, but with time I began to see how its complicity with the culture wars wounded me and other marginalized parts of the body—especially women, people of color, and LGBTQIA+ folks.

I spent the other half of my time in classes that specifically focused on African American history, Asian American history, and the post-colonial experience of Indigenous people from around the world—all told from the perspective of these communities.

I read stories that showed in horrifying detail how patriarchal white supremacy cloaked as Christianity has been used globally as a tool for colonizing and enslaving the bodies and spirits of communities of color. I saw how it was used in America to justify slavery, the Chinese Exclusion Act, Jim Crow segregation, and systems that continue to oppress communities of color today.

If high school history lessons showed me the arrow of Western progress, then these college classes showed me the flesh that arrow sliced through.

As a leader of my Christian fellowship, I started to ask the question: "If we inherited a Western Christianity that has supported systems of oppression, what responsibility do we have to learn from that history and work to dismantle the oppressive systems it set up?" This question did not go over well with my peers. As I saw it, our community was complicit in systems that oppressed parts of the body.

Sometimes, a part of the body of Christ suffers because another part inflicts that suffering. If my lungs are failing because my mouth is chain smoking all day, then I need to stop that harmful behavior. Likewise, if part of the body of Christ is suffering—like people of color, women, and LGBTQIA+ folks—then we need to confess when we are hurting them and change the behaviors and policies that harm them.

Consider folks from different backgrounds who suffer from systemic oppression. What systems have held them down, and what can you do to help push against those systems? Can you relate to their suffering? Do you see ways you can work together toward collective justice?

This devotion was adapted from
"One Body, Many Parts"
by Deborah Jian Lee

GOD'S TABLE
FELICIA FOX

When one of the dinner guests heard Jesus' remarks, he said to Jesus,
"Happy are those who will feast in God's kingdom."
Jesus replied, "A certain man hosted a large dinner and invited many people. When it
was time for the dinner to begin, he sent his servant to tell the invited guests,
'Come! The dinner is now ready.' One by one, they all began to make excuses.
The first one told him, 'I bought a farm and must go and see it. Please excuse me.'
Another said, 'I bought five teams of oxen, and I'm going to check on them.
Please excuse me.' Another said, 'I just got married, so I can't come.'
When he returned, the servant reported these excuses to his master. The master of the
house became angry and said to his servant, 'Go quickly to the city's streets, the busy
ones and the side streets, and bring the poor, crippled, blind, and lame.' The servant said,
'Master, your instructions have been followed and there is still room.' The master said to
the servant, 'Go to the highways and back alleys and urge people to come in so that my
house will be filled. I tell you, not one of those who were invited will taste my dinner.'"
Luke 14:15-24 (CEB)

Jesus loved to tell a good story. All of his stories ended up being about something that wasn't discussed in the story itself. This story found in Luke is really about the kingdom of God, not just a party. We must understand this party to understand the kingdom of God.

We find out that the party is ready, and there are no guests. The first two missing guests must have been men of means. They can afford to buy land and livestock. These purchases may not have been out of necessity or survival since neither seem to test out what they are buying ahead of time. The third just says he can't come. He was just married. Maybe he's letting his wife take the blame for his inability to show up, or maybe he was just partied out and wanted a little time at home.

Each of those who were invited to the party but decided not to come might fit into the "blessed" category. They had been blessed with resources and new relationships. They each had reasons of their own to celebrate. They didn't need to attend this party because they would be invited to another party before too long or they could throw their own party when it better fit their schedule.

So, with an empty banquet hall, the servant is given the job of filling it up. He goes out to the streets and lanes all around town and brings in the poor, crippled, blind, and lame, but there is still more room to be filled. And so the master does the only thing he can. He has the servant go out even further. He sends him out of the town and into the country to bring in anyone he can find to come.

Jesus is trying to tell us who is welcomed in the kingdom of God. It is those on the outside. Those who are sick, suffering, seen as less than, and the outcasts. The homeless and those who are not always welcomed. Those who make their homes in the streets and the country. It isn't just those who seem to be blessed. God is in the business of expanding who is invited in.

If you have ever felt unwelcomed, know you have been invited! You are wanted! You are welcomed in the kingdom of God. There is a place for you here. When God celebrates, God wants you there. So celebrate who you are—you have a party to attend.

This devotion was adapted from
"God's Table"
by Felicia Fox

INTRINSIC HOSPITALITY
J RIEFER

Back in the early 2000's, my church was really into exploring our spiritual gifts; it seemed like "discerning" what your gifts are—attending these seminars, taking these "inventories" with a point system to learn what your gifts were, how God has called you, and how you might be useful—was all the rage. Especially to a bunch of teens and young adults who had spent their formative years steeped in their passionate, evangelical faith.

Much like a personality quiz, we would sit and read 40 or so statements and strongly agree, somewhat agree, somewhat disagree, or strongly disagree. Then we'd count up some numbers, and that would tell us what our gifts were. One morning in Sunday School, a group of us 14-20 year-olds were being introduced to a spiritual gifts inventory. It was exhilarating! Finally, my 17-year-old self would truly know how God could best use me!

It was also hilarious. The test we took told us our spiritual gifts, things we may enjoy or be good at, as well as things that we would not enjoy and would be very very bad at. My friend Paul, who had just turned 15, found out that his main gift was martyrdom. The jokes went on for weeks! My little sister was finally able to put a number to the amount of mercy she had: 0. And my lowest score was always in hospitality.

I have a friend whose personal buzzword is hospitality. Whenever we meet to talk about our church, growth, community activism, antiracist work, and LGBTQIA+ inclusion— hospitality inevitably comes up. I found it a little off-putting at first because, as I said, I'm not super hospitable. But the more that word came up, the more I began to think about the actual meaning of hospitality, beyond nicely cleaned and decorated rooms, woodwick candles, and tea. It turns out I was just approaching the idea of hospitality with too narrow an understanding.

It's time to redefine, to expand our understanding of hospitality and really lean into the concept of intrinsic hospitality.

What is intrinsic hospitality? Where do we start? Let's start with hospitality: the word "hospitality" comes from the Greek word hospes or hostis, which means "stranger" or "the enemy." Weird, right? That's where we get our words for host, hospice, hospital. Hospitality, in its very roots, takes the meaning of a word and turns it on its head. Hospitality is to be hospitable, welcoming, receptive.

The more I thought of and explored the topic of hospitality, the more I discovered that it comes from the humanity within us recognizing, honoring, and caring for the humanity in others. Our actions, our hospitality, pours from what is already innately there. Intrinsic. It is, by our nature, ours. Hospitality sometimes requires doing what is right—what is better—even when it seems like going against what you're "supposed" to.

This devotion was adapted from
"Intrinsic Hospitality"
by J Riefer

The Love Beyond
Our Boundaries
Natalia Terfa

But the legal expert wanted to prove that he was right, so he said to Jesus, "And who is
my neighbor?" Jesus replied, "A man went down from Jerusalem to Jericho.
He encountered thieves, who stripped him naked, beat him up, and left him near death.
Now it just so happened that a priest was also going down the same road.
When he saw the injured man, he crossed over to the other side of the road and went on
his way. Likewise, a Levite came by that spot, saw the injured man, and crossed over
to the other side of the road and went on his way. A Samaritan, who was on a journey,
came to where the man was. But when he saw him, he was moved with compassion.
The Samaritan went to him and bandaged his wounds, tending them with oil and wine.
Then he placed the wounded man on his own donkey, took him to an inn, and took
care of him. The next day, he took two full days' worth of wages and gave them to the
innkeeper. He said, 'Take care of him, and when I return, I will pay you back for any
additional costs.' What do you think? Which one of these three was a neighbor to the
man who encountered thieves?" Then the legal expert said, "The one who demonstrated
mercy toward him." Jesus told him, "Go and do likewise."
Luke 10:29-37 (CEB)

If you have spent any time in the Church, you have likely heard of the parable of the Good Samaritan. As parables go, it's a good one—compelling and powerful.

Jesus is asked what must be done to inherit eternal life—and Jesus answers that the correct answer is written in the law: 1) Love the Lord your God with all your heart and with all your soul and with all your strength and with all your mind, 2) Love your neighbor as yourself. Easy peasy, right? But because we can never just let things be simple, the guy asks Jesus "But who is my neighbor?"

This is a boundary question. Who exactly do I have to love, and when can I stop? When they treat me poorly? When they are foreign? When they don't believe the same things I do? When they don't look like I do or love the way I do?

Jesus commands us to love each other, and just like the guy in this story, we immediately look for ways to put limits on it. The response Jesus gives to this man and his boundary question is the parable of the Good Samaritan—a story about boundary-less love.

A man is robbed, injured, and left on the side of the road. The ones who you would most expect to be helpful—the religious leaders, the churchy people, the faithful worship attenders—they go out of their way to ignore him. They create scenarios in their heads about why this man is unworthy of their attention and care.

But the Samaritan, the one who has been on the outside, has been ignored and ostracized and labeled as a bad foreigner—he is the one who shows the most care, compassion, and love.

He crosses all the boundaries to help. Jesus, as he finishes this parable, doesn't ask the obvious question: "Which one are you?" Instead he asks, "Which... do you think, was a neighbor to the man...?" (v. 36)

The Samaritan man Jesus describes in this parable is even more of an anomaly than just being an outsider who helps. Look at this story again. Look at the way he helps. He bandages the wounds, gives up his spot on his animal (meaning he has to walk instead of ride for the remainder of his journey) and then continues to take care of him at an inn. When he has to continue on his own journey, he gives the innkeeper money to take care of the injured man and says he will come back to pay back whatever additional is spent.

This is above and beyond. It's almost ridiculous in extravagance. This Samaritan man isn't acting in this way for a family member or a friend, but for a complete stranger. I imagine the people listening to this parable were quite shocked. It's just so... much. And then, Jesus says, "Go and do likewise."

The least likely guy is the hero of the story, but part of what makes this story so powerful is that he does the most he can do. Not the least. So what does it mean for us to "go and do likewise"? Who in our world or community or neighborhood is lying on the side of the road, left for dead? And what is the most we can do for that person or group of people?

"Go and do likewise."

This devotion was adapted from
"Loving Beyond Boundaries"
by Natalia Terfa

DELIGHT IN YOUR COMMUNITY

TAMIKA JANCEWICZ
& LAURA KIGWEBA JAMES

The daughters of Jerusalem, friends of Shulamite, respond to the Shulamite's restless heart for her love and say this to her:

> *How is your lover different from any other lover,*
> *you who are the most beautiful of women?*
> *How is your lover different from any other lover,*
> *that you make us swear a solemn pledge?*
> **Song of Solomon 5:9 (CEB)**

The Shulamite woman's friends remind her of her own words of wisdom, of not delighting in love, especially when it does not delight in oneself. But the Shulamite woman ignores her own truth and decides to run around the city searching for a love that is not in search of her.

Maya Angelou writes in her autobiography, The Heart of a Woman: "Sisterhood and brotherhood are conditions people have to work at. It's a serious matter. You compromise, you give, you take, you stand firm, and you're relentless... And it is an investment."

The daughters of Jerusalem are standing firm and reassuring the Shulamite woman that she is already enough and that this relationship is not serving her.

When I was in my discernment period over whether I should stay at my church, I was grateful for the presence of my many sisters and brothers who pointed out the truths that I could not see. They affirmed me, stood with me when they saw I was falling, and encouraged me to pursue opportunities that I could delight in.

We all need to be surrounded by a supportive community. Who is that for you? Who are the people who know the delights of your heart? If you know who they are, send them a note of gratitude. If you are in need of building new friendships, be intentional about the process. Reflect on what you value in friendships and what doesn't serve you in a friendship. Having a strong community in turn nurtures a strong sense of purpose.

This devotion was adapted from
"A New Kind of Love"
by Tamika Jancewicz & Laura Kigweba James

III · LIBERATION

If traditional American Christianity is like falling asleep in a lukewarm bath, then a faith that actively engages with liberation theology is like being showered with ice water; and though you are so bothered by what you know now, you can't imagine ever going back to that lukewarm bath. Your heart breaks, and you are outraged at what evil has been done to the least among us, even in the name of God.

The act of opening oneself up to the lessons of liberation theology is a little bit like lyrics from Weezer's 1994 song "Undone (The Sweater Song)": "If you want to destroy my sweater / Hold this thread as I walk away." There is unravelling to be done.

Once you've begun the path of deconstruction, it's impossible to unsee what was once hidden behind the curtain. Hold onto that thread, walk even further away, and you begin to see the full picture of evil that you've been uncovering.

Liberation theology originated in 1960s Latin America when communities of Catholic clergy and laypeople alike organized to take action against violent political corruption that drove the poor into ever-harsher poverty. Their organizing was fueled by a theology built upon the idea that injustice is a direct result of sin. So, it would naturally follow that taking political action to battle injustice would become crucial to practicing one's faith.

We stand on the shoulders of those giants who came before us in Latin America, who confronted the men and systems in power and began unravelling that thread for us—exposing true evil festering behind every injustice. We continue unravelling, and we find evil deceptively packaged as white Jesus, purity culture, covert "I-don't-see-color" racism, colonization, anti-queerness, xenophobia, Christian exceptionalism. It makes the rich richer and the poor even poorer. It needs you to nod your head and nevermind the agony your neighbor is in.

So, we hand you the thread. Walk. Unravel. Feel righteous anger and let the Spirit, the breath of the Divine within you—let it bring you into the holy fight against injustice.

"Jesus Eraser"
DAVID HAYWARD

CHAPTER 13
Liberation for Black, Brown, & Indigenous Peoples

When I read in the Gospels about Jesus finding worth and dignity in everyone—from tax collectors, to Samaritans, to lepers, to criminals—I know that man Jesus was all about bringing people together, erasing social hierarchies, and giving the best seat to the most unlikely.

Unfortunately, that is not what Christians have continued to do throughout the Church's history. The story of Christianity has become so pervasively whitewashed that too many of us think the only way to encounter God involves being dressed in our Sunday best, hands raised and singing along to the right kind of music, and a cross clearly displayed somewhere on our person.

In this chapter, we share glimpses of our authors navigating their faith lives within a Christian tradition that has been preoccupied for far too long with the whitewashing of its own complicity in perpetuating systems that harm Black, Brown, and Indigenous people.

We invite you in.

KINSHIP
KAITLIN CURTICE

"I was going around the world with the clouds when God
spoke to my thought and told me to ... be at peace with all."
Cochise

Our Thanksgiving story has always been one told about the celebration of newfound friendship between whites and Natives. We pile high our plates of turkey and stuffing, thinking about what it must have been like then, how peaceful that table must have felt. I grew up believing it, too.

Indigenous peoples have ideas around kinship that do not stretch into the white western mind. We live and breathe life in cycles, and we believe that belonging is for every creature under the sun. The ants are our kin, our tribes are our kin, all humanity is an outstretching of kinship. It is a call and responsibility to do everything with care.

Whatever happened on that day that we celebrate as Thanksgiving, what became of it was anything but kinship. Genocide and erasure consumed the land and peoples of Turtle Island, all in the name of God and fortune. But we don't recognize that in our history books. We don't recognize it in our churches.

If we truly believe we are connected to this earth, that we—along with every other creature—get to claim belonging, it should be reflected in everything we do. In other words, we should be gentle, strong people.

We should practice love and care.

We should believe that transformation is possible.

We should hold out hope.

But we should also tell the truth.

America has a lot of wounds, and we've been trying to cover them up with cheap bandages for generations. True kinship cannot be found until we uncover those wounds, take a good look, and heal with the right medicine.

I believe the Church is a really important place to start. And I believe the call right now is to tell the truth.

Creator,
Help us be truth tellers.
Help us come out from behind shadows
to face what is difficult.
Help us experience
what true kinship is,
because you are always
teaching us what it means
to live in community.
Hallelujah.
Amen.

This devotion was adapted from
"Mother Earth & Beloved Belonging"
by Kaitlin Curtice

WHAT DOES IT MEAN TO RISE?

JAZZY HARRISON

Love is patient, love is kind, it isn't jealous, it doesn't brag, it isn't arrogant, it isn't rude, it doesn't seek its own advantage, it isn't irritable, it doesn't keep a record of complaints, it isn't happy with injustice, but it is happy with the truth. Love puts up with all things, trusts in all things, hopes for all things, endures all things.

1 Corinthians 13:4-7 (CEB)

Although slavery took place and ended several hundred years ago, the wounds left behind find new ways to sting everyday. We see firsthand the remnants of oppression in microaggressions, emotional labor, and the senseless murders of unarmed Black people by police.

Freedom from slavery didn't come easy; no one snapped their fingers and ended it all. People had to fight, and many were killed. Black people in this country fought for generations to get where we are today. We recognize the holiday Juneteenth as a time for both celebration and lament.

After the announcement of their freedom, large amounts of formerly enslaved individuals set out to find and reconnect with loved ones across the country. Some set out to seek a place where they would be more welcomed. They set out to search for community.

Black communities all over this country celebrate Juneteenth—the day that commemorates the actual end of slavery in the U.S. (June 19th)—with parades, festivals, and parties. The community that Black people experience by coming together as one to celebrate freedom is nothing short of phenomenal. Despite all the generations of oppression, Black people continue to overcome, and we continue to thrive. So what does it mean to rise?

How beautiful would it be if we all found healthy communities to thrive in? What if we made it a goal to be community to others? In many ways, the love we receive from our communities sets us free. It helps to have this reminder from scripture as love being the Greatest Commandment given to us. How can you love others the way you wish to be loved? How can you show up for the people in your own life?

Reflect on what shameless celebration looks like for you.
How can you show up and shine authentically?

This devotion was adapted from
"Juneteenth: Bound & Escape"
by Jazzy Harrison

COLONIZATION IS ONLY
ONE OF OUR STORIES
ANAYELSI VELASCO-SANCHEZ

"There is a danger in allowing colonization to be the only story of Indigenous lives.
It must be recognized that colonialism is a narrative in which the Settler's power is the
fundamental reference and assumption, inherently limiting Indigenous freedom and
imposing a view of the world that is but an outcome or perspective on that power."
Jeff Corntassel

The act of reclaiming our stories is not so old that being able to do so goes
without question. We're still finding our footing when it comes to standing in
front of whiteness and declaring "That is not true. That is not what happened.
That is not who we are."

For so long, we weren't allowed to tell our own stories. The narratives
about our countries, our people, and even our own bodies were crafted and
controlled by the dominant culture.

Systems of oppression have been held up by stories—the kind that
embedded stereotypes and misconceptions into the consciousness of society
and excused everything to which we have been subjected. But, as necessary
as it is to strengthen our voice as storytellers when it comes to speaking to
dominant culture, that is not why our stories exist.

They don't exist merely as a teaching tool or a challenging lesson for those
outside of our community. They exist for our community.

I once led a workshop called "Storytelling as a Tool for Re-Discovery of
Self and Reunification with Ancestors." After years of leading trainings and
conversations around racial justice that were overwhelmingly for the benefit of white attendees, it was incredibly powerful to lead one in a room that
was solely people of color. The purpose of our time together wasn't to teach

others how to be antiracist, but to allow ourselves to tap into our collective creative imagination as Indigenous and diasporic peoples.

The process of reclamation takes on different shapes depending on who your people are, but as colonized and displaced people, storytelling is crucial. We need to craft meaningful stories, first and foremost, for ourselves. We carry in us an abundance of stories, and it's through our storytelling that we can pursue wholeness and connection.

Practice telling your story. Not as an educational tool or a way to humanize yourself to others, but as a healing and liberating gift for those of us across the diaspora.

Creator, I thank you for the stories I carry. The stories that have remained despite endless attempts at repression and assimilation. I ask that you give me the words and the courage to speak them in order to bless my own people. Amen.

This devotion was adapted from
"We Belong: A Devotional Series for Those in the Borderlands"
by AnaYelsi Velasco-Sanchez

FIGHTING ALONGSIDE THE
JESUS OF LIBERATION

CARLA SOFÍA VARGAS

In Latin America, there are many of us who had the privilege of being born into a family of middle or upper middle class, not to mention the few who belong to five percent of the upper class. Taking into account the historical and generational suffering that our beautiful but wounded region has experienced, it is difficult to take it for granted. Since our "discovery" and our eventual independence, the Latin American countries have gone through wars and dictatorships; we have been raped, looted, and robbed. We (the privileged class) have been made to believe that we deserved our privilege; we have been convinced that the victims of our countries' violent histories are our enemies.

We have also experienced privilege in our Christianity. I confess, at least, that my own environment—thanks to the struggle of my mother and father to give me a better life than the one they lived—made me know a very comfortable gospel. Our family was in many ways the typical Nicaraguan family. A family who go to a beautifully constructed church on Sundays—they dress in their best clothes, arrive when they want, sing, listen to the message, talk to friends and relatives, and then leave; they go to weekday services because they genuinely love God; moms go to Bible Studies; and more than one family member is interested in studying theology. But this typical family is not the reality of most Latin-American Christian families.

If you have not read The Gospel of Solentiname by Ernesto Cardenal, I invite you to do so. This book collected the comments and opinions on the Gospel from a group of peasant farmers belonging to the Solentiname archipelago, located on Lake Cocibolca, the largest in Nicaragua. What wisdom and depth in those pages! Reading it, I came to recognize that these people knew Jesus and his message much better than I did with all my Bible studies and years in the Church. I had never experienced that simplicity and humility that I now see so clearly in the ministry of Jesus. These people did not have a cathedral; they did not have cars to take them to church. Without the burdens of social expectations, material possessions, status, and ego—with the baggage of their difficult experiences and conditions—they offered their all to God.

When Jesus tells the story about the poor widow in Luke 21—the one who offered her last two coins—he ends by saying the following:

"I assure you that this poor widow has put in more than them all. All of them are giving out of their spare change. But she from her hopeless poverty has given everything she had to live on" (Luke 21:3-4, CEB).

I'm sure Jesus was not just talking about economics. For example, I do not imagine Jesus motivating a woman in extreme poverty to give away her twenty pesos a day and not eat (as many pastors do). Jesus understands that those who have nothing have a heart more willing to give—their work, their sweat, their strength, their talents, enthusiasm, and even their few possessions—than the one who has more than enough. Mind you, I am not romanticizing poverty; no one should lack basic needs to see Jesus more closely, but it is true that for those of us who have more than we need—we may have it easier in this life, but it is more difficult for us to actually experience Jesus. So we have to get to know and fight for those who do not have these same privileges, those same people for whom Jesus fought.

"Then he will answer, 'I assure you that when you haven't done it for one
of the least of these, you haven't done it for me.'"
Matthew 25:4 (CEB)

Jesus, I want to know your gospel in the simplest and most real way;
I want to work and fight with and for my siblings who have not
had the same privileges as me.
Amen.

This devotion was adapted from
"The Jesus of Liberation"
by Carla Sofía Vargas

CHAPTER 14
Race in America

One of the most uncomfortable, painful things to learn about and to unlearn from mainstream Christianity is the inherent racism.

In the same way that white supremacy-born racism has stealthily disguised itself as various evils throughout the history of the world—so, too, does the same evil lurk beneath the surface of our theologies, our traditions, our church cultures, our treatment of other religious groups.

When people of faith from marginalized racial groups do the work of deconstruction, we are repeatedly met with an all too familiar grief. Peeling back curtain after curtain to reveal the root evil lurking behind each harmful theology, people of color uncover the truth only to recognize the same stain of white supremacy again and again. Recognizing and dismantling that white supremacism is crucial in the journey towards liberation.

White supremacy has informed and continues to inform the lies of American exceptionalism that directly feeds into our own special brand of Christian exceptionalism in the United States. Christian supremacy is re-packaged white supremacy. So when Black, Indigenous, Latino, and Asian Americans deconstruct our faith, it comes with additional grief as we tally the many ways white supremacy has stolen from us all—especially Black and Indigenous peoples.

Many of our authors throughout this anthology have written their devotions with a lens that helps us see through their perspectives from marginalized racial identities. But we would be remiss not to include even a small chapter dedicated to this particular intersection where faith life meets marginalized racial identities.

Until we dismantle the ways white supremacy has perverted our ideas of God, then our deconstruction and reconstruction remain incomplete and far from liberation.

We invite you in.

Who Will Go with You
in the Aftermath?
Micky ScottBey Jones

In Chapter 21 of John's Gospel, the disciples have gathered together as they often did in the time before the state-sanctioned killing of Jesus. It's been a doozy of a time. The pain is fresh. They are living in what could be considered the aftermath. Some friends are missing. The people who helped before aren't helping now. The person they had been following is dead to most and has appeared a couple of times, but they still aren't sure when, where, how, or if more death and devastation is on the horizon. What are the next steps? It's chaos.

In reading the beginning of John 21, I am reminded of a live recording of the song "Why? (The King of Love is Dead)" by Nina Simone. She is singing it live the day after Rev. Dr. Martin Luther King was murdered in Memphis, Tennessee. The pain is fresh. They are all swimming in the aftermath of the central figure of their movement suffering a violent death. After lamenting the chorus, she takes a break in the song and with anguish in her voice says, "They're killing us all... one by one... we've lost so many... we can't take any more."

Communities continue to experience violence, trauma, and harm. Among the people who followed Jesus. Among the people of the Southern Freedom Movement. Among those of us today whose hearts are awakened to justice and feel the pain of death and trauma all around us.

In the aftermath of those violent or traumatic events, we still have our daily responsibilities and jobs. The disciples still had to feed themselves and were also probably hoping to make a little cash. Which meant they still had to get in the boat and go get some fish. Nina Simone still had to sit at her piano and sing songs and encourage the people.

The disciples had each other to share the tasks and distribute the weight. Nina had her band who worked out the arrangement for a new song of lament.

Have you been living in the aftermath of violence or trauma? Do you find yourself concerned about the violence and/or trauma in your community and how you or others will deal with it? Who are the ones you can call on to help you compose your heart's song of lament or just deal with basic needs in the midst of a difficult time?

God of connection and friendship, of hope and lament, help us in the aftermath of violence and trauma. May we offer one another companionship in daily tasks that still must be done, even in the most devastating of times.

Open us up to sing songs of lament when we gather.

Help us to include our pain and share each other's struggles.

Let us resist the temptation to isolate and instead help us to respond to the Spirit who draws us together.

This devotion was adapted from
"Come Have Breakfast"
by Micky ScottBey Jones

RECEIVING LIFE'S FULLNESS

DEBORAH JIAN LEE

The thief enters only to steal, kill, and destroy. I came so that they could have life—indeed, so that they could live life to the fullest.

John 10:10 (CEB)

I grew up in a mostly white suburb of Chicago where all the "different" kids were relegated to the edges, sometimes tormented, but mostly just dismissed as insignificant. As a Chinese American kid, I interpreted this treatment as a measurement of my self worth. When a kid called me a racial slur and beat me up, I internalized his hatred; part of me began to believe that my ethnicity made me worthless.

It's tempting to blame the kids in my school for this terrible conduct, but perhaps it's more appropriate to look at the culture and institutions that shaped them. Most came from dominant white American Christian culture. Why was there such a huge gap between the gospel's message of inclusion and the way they treated those who were different?

I attribute this gap in part to the fact that we are often more captive to culture than to the teachings of Jesus. Our society validates this idea that people who aren't white, cis, straight, male, able-bodied, and attractive deserve less and can be treated as less.

It wasn't until I began attending a youth group at a Chinese immigrant church that I began to recognize my worth. The gospel makes our value and equality abundantly clear, and the belonging I felt with my new community reinforced that truth. I began to see my life through a radically new lens.

For the first time, I saw people who looked like me at the center of the narrative. At school, we were the Asian wallflowers, invisible to our peers, watching life happen to everyone else. But in youth group, we came alive. We were the cool kids. We were the funny kids. We got to show up, be ourselves, and actually participate in our lives. It shouldn't have been a revelation, but it was.

John 10:10 sets up a powerful juxtaposition between the thief who destroys and the Divine who gives abundant life. In retrospect, it's easy to point out the thieves in my childhood (the bullies, the snobs, the white-centric culture that shaped them) and the life-givers (the haven that embraced me, a worldview that spurred love and equality).

Take a moment to think about your life. Consider the people, places and systems that might operate like thieves, stealing, killing and destroying your spirit. What can you do to put distance between yourself and these harmful spaces?

Now, consider all that gives you life. When do you see yourself coming alive? Who brings out the best in you? Where do you have space to lean into your identity, in all of its complexity and interconnectedness? Let your answers guide you toward more healthy, life-affirming spaces.

The process of deprogramming from our culture's warped metrics of worth takes time and can be painful, but the reward is our liberation.

This devotion was adapted from
"One Body, Many Parts"
by Deborah Jian Lee

WHEN YOU'RE THE ONLY ONE LIKE YOU THERE
ANA YELSI VELASCO-SANCHEZ

*News of him spread even more and huge crowds gathered to listen and to be healed
from their illnesses. But Jesus would withdraw to deserted places for prayer.*
Luke 5:15-16 (CEB)

I always feel a sense of loss when I sell one of my paintings. Each piece takes
hours to create and is often a labor of love and pain—a chance to expel what
is happening inside me onto canvas. There is one piece in particular that I
still struggle with the loss of. She is called "Brown Girl Worshipping," and I
sold her to a white woman who had subjected me to several racial microaggressions over the course of an evening.

I was the artist being showcased in a small bookstore, and she was a friend
of the owner. Friendly and complimentary, she still misnamed me several
times and repeatedly tried to practice her Spanish on me despite me telling
her I am no longer fluent. I found her exhausting and was especially grieved
to hand her "Brown Girl Worshipping"—a piece about the constant struggle
to practice my faith in churches where I am continuously othered. The sad
irony in her loving and buying this painting was not lost on me.

I wanted to say "No, you can't have her. You don't deserve her," but I
needed the money and didn't want to make things awkward. So I said goodbye
to the painting. I think about her and the woman who purchased her often. I
find myself hoping she passes it everyday and is slowly convicted.

How often do those of us on the margins find ourselves in this place?
We are alone even in the presence of others. We make allowances that hurt
us for the sake of others' comfort. We give up pieces of ourselves that we
desperately want to hold onto.

I wish I had told that woman "No." I wish I had said "Yes, but... You need to understand what this painting represents. When you look at it, I need you to know you are complicit. Do you still want her?"

Learning to navigate spaces where our very skin color, the language we speak, and the people we come from subjects us to these inevitable wounds. It is a daily practice in survival and boundary-setting. We can not always exit those spaces. By virtue of choice or circumstance, we end up there, and it becomes about being able to breathe, grow, and flourish despite the limitations of that space. When we feel like we are alone, isolated by our identity, we must find ways to say:

"No"

"Yes"

"I need you to understand..."

"I need you to know..."

Being the only one like us means taking control to ensure the spaces we are a part of, for as long as we need or want to be there, are as safe as possible. It is about being clear about what we are and aren't willing to accept into our lives.

Learn from Jesus, a man alone in his divinity. Jesus knew how to prioritize his needs, sometimes even over those of others. And he knew when to lean into a community and when to step away.

Creator, help me to take courage from the example of Jesus. Remind me daily that though I may be alone or isolated in my identities, like Christ, I have the authority to name my boundaries and to retreat when needed. Protect me from the toxicity of racism and white supremacy. Thank you for reminding me that I have the fortitude to break free—even in the midst of these spaces. Amen.

This devotion was adapted from
"We Belong: A Devotional Series for Those in the Borderlands"
by AnaYelsi Velasco-Sanchez

RUTH THE
MOABITE IMMIGRANT
SAMANTHA FIELD

But Ruth replied, "Don't urge me to abandon you, to turn back from
following after you. Wherever you go, I will go; and wherever you stay, I will stay.
Your people will be my people, and your God will be my God.
Wherever you die, I will die, and there I will be buried.
May the Lord do this to me and more so if even death separates me from you."

Ruth 1:16-17 (CEB)

In the Oxford Jewish Study Bible, the introductory text to Ruth by Adele
Reinhartz points out how the book exists as a contrast to Ezra and Nehe-
miah, boldly and explicitly making the case that "foreigners may be integrated
into the Jewish community." This is a distinct point of view, a story-based
argument for the commands in Deuteronomy and Leviticus to love strangers as ourselves. With such an important case to be made, everything in the
narrative bows down to it, beginning with Ruth's dramatic first words. She
eschews every single scrap of her native identity—where she lives, how she
makes her big decision, her culture, her religion, her entire life: "Wherever
you die, I will die, and there I will be buried." (Ruth 1:17, CEB).

While Ruth's story argues that foreigners should be welcomed into Israel,
it also makes it clear that there is a single right way to go about this. According to the writers, compilers, editors, and curators—retaining any shred of
your own cultural identity isn't possible.

Not only must Ruth throw off her cultural identity, she also has to be the
absolute most perfect immigrant possible, a "model minority" of sorts. After
verbally rejecting her history, she has to give herself over to being noticed as a
productive member of society, someone who is constantly "on her feet" and
barely even rests (2:7). Her willingness to enter Bethlehem's society through

her economic output is praised and directly rewarded, with her agricultural industriousness being the central theme in the second chapter.

Ruth's hard work is noticed by everyone around her, and she's given the benefit of Boaz's protection and even seated by him to eat. Even then, her own hard work is partly erased; when she brings home an ephah of barley, Naomi misattributes all of Ruth's labor to Boaz's hospitality, saying "Blessed be the man who took notice of you" (2:19).

Most disturbingly, Ruth's reproductive life must be given over to the service of her new homeland. Naomi says she only wants Ruth to have a home and be happy, but it's incredibly convenient that the only method of attaining this for her daughter-in-law also results in her retaining some control of Ruth's property and automatically being legally owed her first-born son. The entire community engages in this reproductive oppression—naming Ruth's son and announcing his birth with "A son has been born to Naomi" (4:17).

Reading this final chapter in Ruth, I cannot help but be reminded of what I've seen happening at the U.S.'s southern borders: refugee parents seeking asylum separated from their children. Babies screaming, parents begging to know where their children are. Children disappearing into a rapacious void or being released to an exploitative adoption industry. There's a process in place so horrifically broken that American (and let's not mince words: most likely white, Christian, and straight) couples will receive the "joy" of adopting children who still have mothers desperately searching for them. Mothers, who like Ruth at the end of her story, we will most likely never see or hear from again.

This devotion was adapted from
"Re-Reading Ruth"
by Samantha Field

CHAPTER 15
Capitalism

I had a strange epiphany one day while working on this anthology, and I opened up to my mom about it. I told her I was running around the house, doing laundry, putting dishes in the dishwasher, then upstairs to take a shower and within an hour settled down for a glass of water. It hit me how convenient all of my tasks were. How much longer my day would have been if I needed to fetch my water, boil it, and ration it out for the day.

"I am aware of that all the time," she replied, "and I thank God for it every single day." My mom grew up in rural Zambia with an outhouse and a water pump. She was seventeen when she moved to the U.S., and today she lives in a 4-story home with a roof deck in the heart of Philadelphia. Where she is from, there is still a village with outhouses and water pumps. How can our world be so rich, yet allow for such poverty?

One of my first memories in Zambia is sitting on a bus full of strangers. Someone peeled an orange, and the scent of the fruit filled the cabin. The woman holding the orange split it into halves and kept one for herself. Without introduction, she handed it to the woman on her left. That person took a slice and handed the rest on and on.

I think about that moment often. It also reminds me of something else my mom once told me about the politics of wealth and poverty:

"Poor people give," she said, "rich people buy." But why? Shouldn't it be the other way around?

We live in a capitalist society that exploits the most vulnerable among us. Isn't it our job to do better—to want better—for our friends, our nation, our world?

I started to dream about this world during my personal reformation, a world where we put profits over people, where basic amenities are rights and not privileges. The following authors remind us of how intertwined our Christianity is with capitalism and beg us—no pull us—into a new relationship with both.

We invite you in.

SABBATH & JUSTICE
LYNDSEY MEDFORD

Keep the Sabbath day and treat it as holy,
exactly as the Lord your God commanded.
Deuteronomy 5:12 (CEB)

In the Hebrew Bible, Sabbath is foundational to the community and its relationship to God. We find it throughout the stories, songs, histories, and prophecies of the Hebrew scriptures; and of course, Sabbath is described over and over in the books of the law.

Besides the Exodus story, another list of the Ten Commandments is found in Deuteronomy. In this Sabbath command, the connection between sabbath and justice is made even more explicit. Here, the reason Israel must take a day of rest is focused on the marginalized and on the nation's history of oppression. God did not deliver the Israelites from unending, backbreaking work just so they could impose the same slavery to productivity on themselves or others; they must respect the dignity and value of everyone within their borders—not just the wealthy or powerful.

This is one reason the prophets point to the violation of the Sabbath laws as one of Israel's downfalls (Hosea 2, Amos 8)—because prioritizing productivity over rest and treating people unjustly in the process is a desecration of the image of God in humanity.

For justice seekers, it's easy to talk about rest (or self-care) as time we must take away from our work; but from this perspective, rest is an integral part of our work. It's meant to be foundational—the time signature for the rhythm of our lives. From this perspective, rest is not just a time-out from the real business of being human (work and achievement); instead, all of our work flows out of a place of rest.

If only we treat ourselves as worthy of rest and enjoyment of creation and relationship, allowed to set down our worries about work and the world for one day each week—regardless of whether the to-do list has been ticked—we might ultimately be able to extend that same attitude to others.

That's easy to say and difficult to do; I think that's why Sabbath is a command instead of just a nice idea. Sometimes, we need to practice living as if something were true before we can believe it for ourselves. If we always wait until we are really convinced we have done enough of our work before we "deserve" to rest, we would never quite get there. If we hope that God's peace and love are already breaking into our imperfect world but never take the time to celebrate God's presence already with us—our hope remains an abstraction, not a reality.

Today, human beings are still exploited for their labor without being ensured the dignity, health, relationship, and happiness that come with a day of rest. Living in the spirit of the Sabbath also means advocating for a living wage and adequate time off for all. But it also means taking, if possible, sabbath for ourselves: claiming the right of every person to have time set apart simply for being.

We can't oppose the forces of dehumanization by just working harder. Our true power to oppose them comes from living in light of the truth about ourselves and others: that we are all worthy and beloved just for being God's children—not for being right, or for doing work, or for earning other people's favor.

It takes humility to live as a child. I need God's power to let go of the comforting checklist of rules that might make me acceptable. I am re-learning childlike trust to wait for, listen for, and believe God's answer: Live in belovedness. Live in radical self-acceptance. Live in love for this jagged, wounded world around you. Live out of stillness, practicing presence. Live as a witness to grace.

This devotion was adapted from
"The Burnout's Guide to Being Human"
by Lyndsey Medford

CAPITALISM DOES NOT BELONG IN OUR FAITH
SueAnn Shiah

There are people who think that godliness is a way to make money! Actually, godliness is a great source of profit when it is combined with being happy with what you already have.

We didn't bring anything into the world, so we can't take anything out of it; we could be happy with food and clothing. But people who are trying to get rich fall into temptation. They are trapped by many stupid and harmful passions that plunge people into ruin and destruction.

The love of money is the root of all kinds of evil. Some have wandered away from the faith and have impaled themselves with a lot of pain because they made money their goal.

But as for you, man of God, run away from all these things. Instead, pursue righteousness, holy living, faithfulness, love, endurance, and gentleness.
1 Timothy 6:5-11 (CEB)

We live in a society that has normalized the results of capitalism; we live as if greed is good. Pervasive in the Christianity of the West is the idea that the most just way to run a society is an economic system built on the love of money.

In the passage from 1 Timothy, we are warned not to trust teachers and faith leaders who say that 'godliness is a means of gain.' The greatest gift that righteousness and godliness will give us is contentment and peace that comes not from an accumulation of the perfect amount of belongings or wealth, but from faith and trust that God our great provider loves and cares for us.

We must be vigilant to reject within ourselves the love of money and things, as well as to cultivate a heart that desires to see the hungry fed, the prisoner set free, and abundant singing, dancing, and joy.

When I was a teenager, one of my best friends was an extremely generous person who was always treating people to coffees or lunches—something I never did, though I had the expendable income. Once, I asked how and why she was always treating people, and she told me that the joy on people's faces, seeing how happy it made them made it easy for her.

Our generosity is and will always be connected to those around us in our communities, friends, and families. When we hoard, it is these same people who we hurt and push away. Our liberation is bound up with one another, and without these relationships with God and those made in the image of God—we will not be able to desire, love, and pursue righteousness and justice.

This devotion was adapted from
"Sparking Joy & Shunning Fear"
by SueAnn Shiah

When Wealth Begets Evil
Michelle Henrichs

When the king's order and his new law became public, many young women were gathered into the fortified part of Susa under the care of Hegai. Esther was also taken to the palace to the care of Hegai, the one in charge of the women.
Esther 2:8 (CEB)

In chapter 2 of Esther, King Ahasuerus, wealthy and powerful ruler of Persia, is rounding up the virgins to find his new queen. But this is no Cinderella story. There is no fairy godmother to explain to these girls, in their many languages, what is happening. There are no friendly mice and twittering birds to accompany the girls as they undergo their beautification for the king's judgment.

While Mordecai seems to have high enough standing at court to freely move about and inquire after Esther, this would have been a rarity for other fathers. As for Esther and the other girls, they would not have had knowledge of anything going on outside the harem.

At essentially the age of puberty, because girls were married soon after, royal officers or military men came to their homes and public places and took them away from their families to serve powerful men. If only this was just an ancient story.

We don't like to talk about it, but this is also our story today. One of the dark sides of our American wealth and power that we do not talk about: the trafficking of young girls and boys. Statistically, around 49% of trafficked children begin being used for sex between the ages of twelve and seventeen, with 10% being younger than eleven.

Individually, we cannot stop the powerful from rounding up the virgins, but we can initiate the beginning of the end by educating ourselves. We can name this injustice out loud. The ancient story is silent about how the people of Persia responded. This doesn't need to be our story. We are called to break the silence.

> *God of the stolen and forgotten:*
> *For those who find themselves in the dark captivity of human-trafficking and work conditions that are dangerous and pay unlivable wages, we pray that you would be their encouragement until freedom and justice come.*
> *We pray that the bright glare of your light would expose where power is manipulated and money is valued more than humanity.*
> *Teach us not to look away but to speak against these inhumanities.*
> *Lord, give us hearts to care and a desire to act.*
> *Amen.*

This devotion was adapted from
"When They Rounded Up the Virgins"
by Michelle Henrichs

CALLED TO REST
& GIVE UP POWER
SUEANN SHIAH

The heavens and the earth and all who live in them were completed. On the sixth day
God completed all the work that he had done, and on the seventh day God rested from
all the work that he had done. God blessed the seventh day and made it holy, because on
it God rested from all the work of creation.

Genesis 2:1-3 (CEB)

The more things we own, the more our things own us. We often consider the extension of our efforts to gain power in the world of space, but plainly put: we trade our labor for money, then this money is converted into belongings and land—all in the hopes of making our lives easier. But we are less likely to reflect on the reality of the inverse, which can be summed up as "mo' money mo' problems."

God's work is never finished, but on the seventh day, God declared the work of creation finished. Then God sanctified it, made it holy, and set the seventh day aside for rest. In our busy lives of toil and constant work, it is rare to find room for rest, for self-care, for a holy sabbath. If our belongings require so much time and maintenance from us that we are unable to rest, perhaps we might need to downsize the size and quantity of our belongings.

For some of us, our ambitions drive us to accomplish. And we feel that in order to get the edge that we need to accomplish our goals, we must work without ceasing. For some of us, our desire for social justice drives our work; there are so many causes, organizations, and individuals who need us, and we feel as if we cannot set aside time to rest when there is so much good work to be done. No matter what the work is, it is still important to rest.

Whether we desire to accumulate, to have dominion over the land, or to help and save—these desires are rooted in the hope that we could be like

God (one that is all powerful, has all, and/or is able to save all people). We may justify to ourselves—how much more useful would a little more time, a little more money, or a little more power be?

God called us to work just as God called us to rest, but if our work and toil is only in the pursuit of accumulating more wealth and more resources, we will find ourselves broken at capitalism's altar instead of finding joy in participating in the bountiful harvest that God has prepared for us.

And if our work and toil is in the pursuit of "saving" the needy, then we have put ourselves in the place of Jesus and made ourselves saviors, elevating ourselves above other humans, when we are simply needy humans as well.

How is God calling you to rest and to know that your worth and value is not fixed at your productivity? If setting aside intentional time to rest and participate in Sabbath-keeping means losing some income, you might consider how to include your community to share this burden together.

How can you make space for resting, for the things that spark joy in your life?

Pray for the joy of the Lord to fill your heart and replace your worries. Pray that the need for "usefulness" be replaced with peace and rest.

This devotion was adapted from
"Sparking Joy & Shunning Fear"
by SueAnn Shiah

CHAPTER 16
Liberation for All

Jo Luehmann talks about a vision of heaven on earth that I didn't really understand until I was in the middle of working on this book. She believes and preaches that if we can free ourselves from the binds of capitalism, racism, ableism, purity culture, misogyny, homophobia, transphobia—all of those evil monsters that seek to dehumanize us—then we have a shot at a utopia that is at one with the God we discovered when at first we believed.

Heaven on earth, huh?

That phrase, that image of having heaven on earth, is audacious because it has so much faith in us—we the people who are inherently fallible. That statement leads with hope for a society hell-bent on destruction, chaos, and self-inflicted wounds. It is a Word of Love where most of us have decided we don't have eyes to see or ears to hear.

What an audacious idea. Maybe even impossible. But then I think… There are two things that I read about the most in the Bible: love and hope. What a radical thing, hope. Coupled with love, hope makes this impossible-sounding work of creating a justice-centered heaven on earth, where everyone is liberated from oppression, seem possible. And if we can hope for it, then surely we can work for it.

We invite you in.

THE LIBERATION
OF PENTECOST
REV. LENNY DUNCAN

When Pentecost Day arrived, they were all together in one place. Suddenly a sound from
heaven like the howling of a fierce wind filled the entire house where they were sitting.
They saw what seemed to be individual flames of fire alighting on each one of them.
They were all filled with the Holy Spirit and began to speak in other languages as the
Spirit enabled them to speak.

Acts 2:1-4 (CEB)

Church is weird. It's full of weird people doing weird, 1800-year-old things
(no matter how many lights or fog machines there are up front). But it is
meant to be set apart—a bastion of the Kin-dom of God, a place where
systemic racism and white supremacy are dismantled. A place where transphobia and homophobia fall apart when met with the power of the ancient
sacraments. Where misogyny is laid bare and exposed for what it is: the naked,
raw nerve of desperate attempts at male dominance.

But it's also supposed to be a place where time is warped and moments
can stretch on in complete connection with the Divine forever. Where you
are out of lockstep with the calendar of the world and find a new way to
march out of the capitalist calendar's demands.

The Church calendar is an anarchist middle finger shoved in the face of
the imperialist cycle of the year. It is anti-empire and life-giving. All of this—
church weirdness and the anti-empire nature of the Church calendar—brings
us to Pentecost. But what the fuck is a Pentecost?

The day of Pentecost marks the day it all turned around—the birthday
of the Church. Not the oppressive and, frankly, gross Church many of us
have known. No, it is the birth of a grassroots movement of peoples on the

margins, people who are about to embark on the greatest adventure of their lives and change the entire world.

God chooses to announce the Church in wonderful Black, White, Asian, and Brown diversity. It is Middle Eastern in accent and Mediterranean in disposition. There is, like, one European honorable mention: "and visitors from Rome" (Acts 2:10, CEB). God expresses Godself and the birth of God's Church on earth in diversity. It is pluralistic and rich. It is in many languages and cultures. It is expressed through the mosaic of human experience and doesn't reflect the monolithic churches we often gather in today.

This church thing. This Pentecost thing. This Holy Spirit thing. It is so otherworldly. It is so disruptive and powerful that when it presents itself to the world, people think you're on something. Yes, there are some who will recognize something "other" is happening here and will be blown away or confused. And there will be some who think "Those people have lost their fucking minds—that's not how God shows up."

Pentecost is the day all that started to happen in human history, and it's still unfolding today.

The Spirit wants to make love to us and with us. She wants to be joined in our work for liberation. She wants to give you the words when you stand up to your church leadership and explain that being queer-affirming is the only way forward. Or that dismantling white supremacy and creating antiracist spaces is the call of the Church in the 21st century. She will bolster you like Peter and help you declare, like Mary did, that the resurrection is real. That death is defeated, and the brown man you thought you lynched and hanged from a tree is alive!

That is Pentecost. It is the thing that makes you want the Church to be better. It's why you would come back after it kicked your ass—because you aren't going to let that happen to anyone else. It is why you march, why you pray. It is the day that you were given access to all the gifts Jesus had and more.

We should party on this day. We should celebrate on this day. We should stand before thousands and give a full-throated cry of freedom.

We have been given access to the Spirit's disruptive power; and it is a working part of our minds and spirits, whether we acknowledge it or not.

Liberating Jesus, you sent us the Holy Spirit so we can disrupt the world
and all its fuckery. Help me to be brave enough to tap into that
power and lead others to liberation.
Amen.

This devotion was adapted from
"What the Hell Is a Pentecost?"
by Rev. Lenny Duncan

GETTING TO KNOW
THE JESUS OF LIBERATION
CARLA SOFÍA VARGAS

Ironically, in the church where I grew up, the life of Jesus was almost never mentioned in the sermons. For some reason the pastor usually chose some chapter of the Old Testament or some Pauline letter, then ended up talking about the love of God despite our mistakes and infidelities, and only then about how He sent his only begotten son to die for us. So during the general church assembly, his death on the cross was the only reference made about Jesus.

This felt very different from my experience in Sunday school, where children were always told about Jesus—the friend of the rejected, the miracle worker, that man who loved his disciples and healed the sick. And, of course, these stories were always accompanied by a coloring activity.

So what happened, that our perspective of Jesus changes as we grow, and we stop seeing him as more than just "the Savior who came to die for us"? Because if we are honest with ourselves, the redeeming and sacrificial aspect of Jesus is often the one that predominates the collective imagination of many Christians. The Jesus who was a man, friend, and revolutionary is sometimes rarely the protagonist in the pulpits or circles of Church studies. We are missing a lot.

When one reads the story of Jesus in the Gospels, it is easy to fall in love with the life and struggle of that man who spent every second of his ministry loving the unprotected, fighting against injustice, and going against every system of oppression—moral, religious, social, and political—in his speeches, teachings, and (above all) his actions.

If every person is a beautiful canvas of different identities (for example, I celebrate that I am a woman, a Latina-mestiza, Nicaraguan, lesbian, and Christian), why don't we think the same of Jesus? Why do we only keep one aspect of his ministry and his life? I would be very upset if the people who know me accept one of my identities and deny the rest. In my case, if you want to be my friend, you have to accept and recognize all my identities. Yes, it's all or nothing. Because I am one hundred percent in each of them.

Knowing Jesus and knowing ourselves in totality is one of the most powerful and, above all, liberating experiences we could ever experience.

Jesus, help me to know you and to know me in a more intimate and complete way.
I want to celebrate every part of your story and mine.
Amen.

This devotion was adapted from
"The Jesus of Liberation"
by Carla Sofía Vargas

Collective Liberation

Rozella Haydée White

God's second act of love was Jesus, God embodied as human. I am an incarnation-biased Christian. This means that I find the most power and love of God in the incarnation and not in the death and resurrection. There is no greater love than to be with another. In Jesus, we see a God who loves us so passionately that God chose to embody love in the human form and go through life with us.

Jesus is liberation personified. Jesus brings to bear the inbreaking of a new world order, one that is marked more by the Beatitudes than by the powers and structures of the world. Jesus turns everything upside-down and inside-out. The things we thought we knew (the Law) become further understood through a different lens when we encounter a new life in Christ that is defined by grace (the gospel).

We often think of liberation as the freedom from physical bondage, which it most certainly can be. But God's liberation in Jesus is about physical, emotional, mental, and spiritual freedom. God cares about the WHOLE person and the ways that we live and love one another.

"I am not free while any woman is unfree, even when her shackles are very different from my own." —audre lorde

Here's the thing about liberation: It can only be experienced individually if it is shared collectively. In Jesus, we see that God was not simply concerned with the individual, but with the collective. Liberation is the act of creating freedom that can be experienced holistically. When our thoughts are free and our feelings are free and our bodies are free and our souls are free, WE are free. When WE are free, the world is free.

The work of liberation is not work of kindness. It is work of justice. Of a fierce and fiery cry for equity so that all may experience abundant life. The work of liberation is ongoing. It's less about a one-time act and more about a lifestyle. Isn't that what Jesus modeled? A lifestyle?

To be a follower of Christ is to be a seeker and creator of liberation. Liberation brings healing, and God wants us to be made well and be whole. The signs that we are in bondage to sin are all around us. And when I use the term sin in this context, I am specifically talking about a fundamental condition of being inwardly focused and disconnected from God, from others, and from ourselves. This is sin. This is brokenness. This is the condition from which we are seeking liberation.

Love cannot exist without liberation, without freedom.

This devotion was adapted from
"Love Big"
by Rozella Haydée White

CPSIA information can be obtained
at www.ICGtesting.com
Printed in the USA
LVHW040555161221
706260LV00010B/1129